CAREER OPPORTUNITIES IN ART

CAREER OPPORTUNITIES IN ART

Susan H. Haubenstock
and
David Joselit

Facts On File Publications
New York, New York • Oxford, England

To Edna S. Hirsh,
who cultivated our love of art.

Career Opportunities in Art

copyright © 1988 by Susan H. Haubenstock and David Joselit

Library of Congress Cataloging-in-Publication Data

Haubenstock, Susan H.
  Career opportunities in art.

  Bibliography: p.
  Includes index.
  1. Art—Vocational guidance—United States.
I. Joselit, David.   II. Title.
N6505.H35 1988   702.3'73   87-22212
ISBN 0-8160-1398-5 (hc)
ISBN 0-8160-1982-7 (pbk)

British CIP data available on request

Printed in the United States of America

10 9 8 7 6 5 4 3 2 1

CONTENTS

SECTION 8—ART-RELATED BUSINESSES

SECTION 9—APPENDIXES

ACKNOWLEDGMENTS

The authors gratefully acknowledge the assistance of the following individuals who provided information for this book:

Joan Arenberg, art consultant; Barry R. Bauman, Chicago Conservation Center; Peter Blum, print edition producer; Valerie Bove, Institute of Contemporary Art, Boston; Ann Boyd, Roy Boyd Gallery; Terence Brown, Society of Illustrators; Donna Cooper, Mobil Chemical Company; Jim Dady, Massachusetts Council on the Arts and Humanities; Richard Flood, Barbara Gladstone Gallery; Hal Foster, art critic; Gary Garrels, DIA; Merrie Good, Chase Manhattan Bank; Chriss Holderness, Institute of Contemporary Art, Boston; Abigail Housen, art educator; Jennifer D. Josselson, Christie's; Jeffrey Kline, Kline Art Supply; Peter Krueger, Christie's; Diane Mandel, custom framer; Kathy Morrill, artist; Carla Munsat, *Art New England*; Helaine Posner, University of Massachusetts Art Gallery; Sharon Siegel, Albany School of Visual Arts; Barbara Strongin, Christie's; Michael Tarantino, Massachusetts Council on the Arts and Humanities; Bernard Ungerlieder, artist; Anne Young, Christie's; and William Zamprelli, Eagle Transport.

PREFACE

Purpose

Career Opportunities in Art is a comprehensive listing of jobs for people interested in the art world. Eight major categories of careers are presented, and 75 different positions are described. Job descriptions are detailed and include information on duties, salaries, prerequisites, employment and advancement opportunities, relevant organizations and special advice on getting into the desired field. The book is intended both for those who are seeking entry-level jobs and for more experienced people who are thinking of changing careers.

Sources of Information

Research for the book included numerous interviews with professionals in various fields, as well as information obtained from professional organizations, the federal government, and library research. In addition, coauthor David Joselit contributed his own experience and expertise as a museum staff member and art journalist.

The job descriptions are generalized from the many actual jobs we reviewed. Certainly, job content, salaries and growth potential vary from one organization to another, based on the organization's size, geographic location and philosophy; we have noted some of these variations within the job descriptions in this book.

Organization of Material

This book has nine sections. The first eight cover different fields that employ many people in art-related positions; the ninth consists of appendixes listing educational institutions, trade schools, scholarhips, organizations and associations, and a bibliography.

All the positions covered in the book are intended for people with studio art and/or art history backgrounds and interests, often combined with other skills. We have not gone into the field of design, which has been covered in several of the books listed in the bibliography, but have instead provided exhaustive presentations of careers in museums, art galleries, funding agencies, auction galleries, art journalism and the like. Many of the jobs described here have not been presented in other books on art careers, and we hope to give the reader new and different job possibilities to consider.

Explanation of Job Descriptions

Each job description follows a basic format and is complete within itself, so the reader does not need to refer to other parts of the book to get a complete picture of a given job. As a result, the reader may note some repetition from job description to job description.

Jobs are listed by the predominant title, followed by a career profile that summarizes a job's major duties, alternate titles, salary range, prospects for employment and advancement, and prerequisites, including education, experience and special skills. The career ladder diagram shows a typical career path, including positions leading to and growing from each job. If a job is at the entry level, "student" is listed as preceding it.

The position description notes the typical duties and responsibilities of the job and the environment in which the job occupant functions. The section on salaries explains income ranges and notes factors that may affect them, such as individual skills, size of the employing organization or geographic location. Salary ranges are based on averages, and readers may find positions that pay more or less than the figures given in this book.

Readers should particularly note the sections on employment prospects and advancement prospects, which can lend some reality to the idea of working in an attractive but often overcrowded or underpaid field. Exciting-sounding jobs may be difficult to obtain, while jobs that are relatively easy to get may be dead ends. These are important considerations for a job seeker.

The education section describes the academic requirements of the job. These can range from no formal requirements to graduate degrees and specialized training.

The experience and skills section describes work experiences that are necessary in order to obtain the job and cites personal qualities and abilities that successful candidates should possess.

The section on organizations and associations suggests groups that might be useful to the jobseeker by providing support, information, education and the opportunity to make professional contacts. Where there are no relevant organizations or associations, there is no listing.

Finally, there are tips for entry, which consist of advice from professionals in the field on how to get a foot in the door of your desired career.

Appendixes

Appendix I lists 71 colleges and universities in the United States that offer programs in art therapy, art conservation, arts administration and arts management. As noted in Appendix I, nearly all colleges in this country have courses of study in art and art history, so we have not listed schools with these majors; any good college handbook will provide this information.

Appendix II lists 250 trade, industrial and vocational schools that train artists in studio art and design.

Appendix III contains information on art scholarships, fellowships, grants and loans.

Appendix IV lists organizations and associations that can be useful to those wishing to pursue any of the careers covered in this book.

Finally, Appendix V is a bibliography listing periodicals and books that provide additional information on the jobs described here.

INTRODUCTION

FINDING A CAREER IN ART

You enjoy art. You like the freedom to express yourself, and you are excited by the opportunity to create something new. You have taken art classes, you have mastered new skills and you have seen your own abilities grow. You have gone to museums and galleries and have been challenged and inspired by the work of other people.

You have decided to make your career somewhere in this world of art. Despite visions of penniless artists and warnings that you can't make a living at it, you believe that you can find a place in the art community.

And it can be done. With careful study and planning, hard work and determination, some flexibility and the right information, you can find a job in the art world and begin to build a career.

Romance vs. Reality

Certainly, you have chosen a difficult field. Many thousands of art graduates each year join the search for the dream job—a well-paid position at a prestigious museum, let's say, or the post of critic for an important art magazine. Those jobs are out there, of course, but the competition for them is fierce, and the salaries can be less than what one might hope for. The problem, then, at the beginning of your career planning is to take a clear-eyed look at what jobs are available and what kind of life you can expect to live while occupying such jobs.

There are many different aspects to consider. Exactly how closely related to art must the job be? Will you be happy only if you're a portrait painter? Could you enjoy teaching art, or writing about it, or selling other people's works? Would you be happy reviewing artists' grant proposals or selling art supplies? In general, it can be said that jobs that are less closely related to the act of creating art are easier to get. That is, it is generally easier to find work as a framer than as, say, an illustrator.

Income is another prime consideration. Are you willing to start at the bottom, in a low-paying job? If you begin as an art gallery receptionist, for example, you can get a foot in the door of the gallery business.

Upward mobility may be important to you. Do you hope to get into a career where there is a significant opportunity for you to be promoted to higher positions? If so, you might be interested in museum work or in a job with a funding organization, rather than in the fields of art therapy or conservation.

Some careers require lengthy preparation; an art history instructor, for instance, usually needs a doctorate. A framer, on the other hand, can train on the job and become proficient within months.

There are jobs in which it is important to be able to deal well with people, such as customer service positions in auction galleries. And there are jobs in which that ability is less important—say, as a preparator at an art gallery.

Finally, there are jobs that are best for risk-taking entrepreneurial types—freelance careers, for example—and jobs that offer more security, such as elementary and high school art teaching.

All these considerations—and perhaps more, based on your personal needs—are vital to your choice of the right career for yourself. It is important to learn as much as you can by reading material on career planning and on the art world in general, and by talking to people in your fields of interest. And it is equally important to listen to yourself and to be honest about your career wants and needs.

The Most Promising Fields

Because many art career areas are so competitive, it may be helpful to note where jobs can be found most easily. In general, the commercial, profit-making side of the art world is more open to newcomers than the nonprofit side. It is easier to find work in a gallery than in a museum, and it is easier to get a job at an auction house than in a school art department. Business-related art careers are more plentiful, especially within a successful and growing concern. Government agencies and museums depend on appropriations and donations for funds, and they tend to hire fewer people and to have less to pay them with.

It is a paradox that the image of the "artistic" person is of someone who is distant from the constraints of the business world, incapable of dealing with practicalities. In fact, even an independent fine artist needs practical, real-world skills to succeed at making a living in art. Everyone needs sales skills—to make contacts with potential employers or customers, to achieve a promotion, to get people interested in a new idea or pet program. Any background that combines art and business will likely provide good experience. And any "artistic" person who can appreciate and master some basic marketing and other business skills will have a lifelong advantage over those who don't have such skills.

The Importance of Focus

Regardless of what career you eventually choose as your goal, you can improve your chances of entering the career you want by focusing your energies on it. It really is unimportant how competitive a field is; if you focus your effort on becoming the best prepared, most qualified candidate for the job, your prospective employer will have no choice but to hire you.

How do you achieve this? The first step is to research the careers that interest you until you can make an intelligent choice. Your research should include plenty of reading about the career and the people in it; check books, periodicals and newspapers. In addition, you should check with organizations and associations of people in the field for information they can provide. Attend meetings of such organizations and speak to people in your area of interest; they can give you the best and most current information on the field and how to enter it.

Through your research you will learn how other people have prepared to enter the career field to which you aspire and what qualifications employers seek when they are filling jobs. Then your mission is simple: to focus your efforts on becoming the best candidate for the job you want. It may require formal education or an apprenticeship; it may steer you toward a certain volunteer or summer job rather than another one. It may help you to select business courses as electives while you major in art; it may lead you to look for a specific part-time or summer job to get some experience. The bottom line is to know what you want and to set out in a determined way to get it.

Flexibility

What if you just aren't that focused on a specific career? There is something to be said for flexibility, too. Perhaps you feel that you want to work in the art world in some way, but the specific job is not that important to you. Without a strong focus, you may feel a bit adrift, but you have the advantage of being able to select from a wide variety of possibilities.

You might choose a line of work, such as art journalism, and just take any entry-level opening that comes up—perhaps something in the circulation department or in advertising sales. Or you might take a secretarial job in an art-related business in order to learn more about it and see if it's right for you.

Free-lancing

Another way to look at the career picture is to consider self-employment or free-lancing. It takes a certain kind of outlook to feel comfortable working for yourself; many people prefer to get some experience working for others before setting up on their own. It may take some money to get started in a business. A free-lancer can have dry spells between jobs, and income may be erratic. But there are numerous people who enjoy working for themselves, setting their own hours (to some degree) and choosing the assignments they take on (once they become established).

Several art careers lend themselves to free-lancing. A fine artist, for example, is really a sort of free-lancer. Illustrators, independent curators, art consultants, art journalists, conservators and preparators can all work on a free-lance basis. Self-employment is the norm for gallery owners, print publishers, art school directors and custom framers, among others.

A Note on Geography

It is important to consider where you can find art jobs. Many of the positions art graduates seek are available only in large cities—particularly in New York, which is the art capital of the United States. The largest number of art galleries, auction houses, museums and funding organizations is in New York. Other important cities for art jobs are Washington, Boston, Chicago, Atlanta, Houston, Dallas, Los Angeles and San Francisco.

But many art-related jobs are available in a wide variety of communities. Art galleries exist in numerous small towns and resort areas. Quite a few museums are located in smaller cities. Art teachers work in schools throughout the country, and framers can be found in most towns.

Geography should be an important issue for you to think about. The major cities offer more art positions and have more workers in the field of art, while the smaller towns may provide equally good jobs with less competition and a more relaxed life-style.

Accepting the Challenge

The same qualities that attracted you to the world of art in the first place can be channeled to help you find the career you want. Use your vision to choose your goal, and use your creativity to make your way toward that goal. You have chosen a challenging and exciting field; challenge yourself to do your very best to find the right job and go after it with everything you have. This is the only way to achieve the satisfaction of working in the fascinating and inspiring art world.

SECTION 1
WORKING ARTISTS

COMMERCIAL ARTIST

CAREER PROFILE

Duties: Prepare artwork according to specifications

Alternate Titles: Graphic Artist, Designer, Advertising Artist

Salary Range: $15,000 to $45,000

Employment Prospects: Good

Advancement Prospects: Poor

Prerequisites:
    Education—Bachelor's degree in art or commercial art school diploma required; master's degree in art helpful

    Experience—On-the-job training or co-op program background useful

    Special Skills—familiarity with computer graphics; typesetting; camera work

CAREER LADDER

```
┌─────────────────────────┐
│     Art Supervisor      │
└─────────────────────────┘

┌─────────────────────────┐
│    Commercial Artist    │
└─────────────────────────┘

┌─────────────────────────┐
│      Junior Artist      │
└─────────────────────────┘
```

Position Description

The title of Commercial Artist is used here to cover a wide range of art careers, from graphics to advertising art to free-lance work. In essence, a Commercial Artist uses various art skills in the service of a business concern. Commercial Artists work in product design, in publishing houses, for newspapers and magazines, for advertising agencies and departments in large companies, and in many other areas.

A beginning or junior Commercial Artist can expect to learn and use numerous art skills and techniques to fulfill the requirements of a particular job—for instance, to design the typography and layout of a brochure, corporate annual report or book jacket and to prepare artwork to illustrate it. As time goes on and the Commercial Artist becomes more experienced, he or she may expect to have more input into the creative makeup of assigned projects—to supervise the overall look of a series of advertisements or to choose color combinations for packaging materials.

Commercial art can be exciting or routine and repetitive, depending on the company and the kind of work assigned. It is, of course, different from working as an independent fine artist, since other people, not the artist, are in control of the final work.

Many Commercial Artists work on a free-lance basis, marketing their skills to organizations that have no in-house artists or that need extra help with artwork from time to time. This gives the artist more control over the work, although the client, of course, assigns and specifies the tasks to be done.

Salaries

Though starting salaries tend to be low, good Commercial Artists can increase their incomes fairly quickly and can supplement them with free-lance jobs, if they wish. An entry-level salary might range from $15,000 to $20,000, and salaries can go as high as $45,000 for those with proven skills.

Employment Prospects

Currently, employment prospects in commercial art are good, with computer graphics leading the way to an expansion in the number of positions available. Of course, those who wish to enter the field need to be up-to-date on the latest computer technology as it applies to art, graphics and design in order to take advantage of these new positions.

Advancement Prospects

Chances for advancement in commercial art are relatively limited because there are many long-term employees in this career field. Though artists may move more frequently between advertising agencies or magazines, for instance, they tend to move laterally, not upward to supervisory positions. However, willingness to relocate may improve a Commercial Artist's chances to advance in the career.

Education

Commercial Artists may have either bachelor degrees in fine arts or diplomas from commercial art schools, depending on the requirements of individual companies. Typically, the larger the company, the more important it is to have a college degree, and a master's degree is preferable to most very large firms.

Experience and Skills

Any kind of commercial art experience that can be gained while in school—particularly co-op education programs and opportunities for on-the-job training in part-time work—is extremely valuable when it comes time to find a job in the field. Even volunteer work on a college newspaper or yearbook can be helpful.

At the present time, a complete familiarity with computer graphics and computer art capability is essential to the commercial art jobseeker. In addition, all the skills taught in commercial art programs should be in place—typesetting, camera work, etc.

Organizations and Associations

There is no central organization for Commercial Artists, but such groups as the Society of Illustrators (see Appendix IV) provide services that may be useful to workers in this field.

Tips for Entry

The two keys to entry into commercial art are familiarity with the latest advances in computer art and the acquisition of any type of on-the-job experience, no matter on what level.

CONSERVATOR

Duties: Prepare, clean, reconstruct, retouch and document artwork

Alternate Title: Restorer

Salary Range: $20,000 to $30,000

Employment Prospects: Good

Advancement Prospects: Good

Prerequisites:

Education—Master's degree in art history or art conservation; specialized training in restoration

Experience—Apprenticeship in restoration

Special Skills—Eye training, drawing and painting, science background

```
┌─────────────────────────────┐
│                             │
│     Senior Conservator      │
│                             │
└─────────────────────────────┘

┌─────────────────────────────┐
│                             │
│        Conservator          │
│                             │
└─────────────────────────────┘

┌─────────────────────────────┐
│                             │
│    Assistant Conservator    │
│                             │
└─────────────────────────────┘
```

Position Description

A Conservator is responsible for the treatment of art work—to repair damage, preserve quality and document the status of the work. This involves preparatory steps, such as uncrating and photographing the work, followed by cleaning, retouching, structural repair and/or other operations.

Major museums employ Conservators, as do commercial operations that provide conservation and restoration services to the public.

Conservation and restoration is a specialized field, and it takes considerable training to prepare for this career. The Conservator must be educated and have practical training in fine arts and art history, and in addition must have a considerable mastery of physics and chemistry in order to understand and work with art materials.

Salaries

Salaries for art conservators range from $20,000 to $30,000 per year.

Employment Prospects

Employment prospects for Conservators are very good. This is a field that is growing as collectors become increasingly aware of the need to preserve and care for the artwork they own. In addition, there are new areas, such as photo conservation, that are wide open for those interested in pursuing a career in restoration.

Advancement Prospects

Conservators can expect to advance to supervisory positions in this career fairly readily. Again, the expansion within the field will continue to open up new positions as time goes on. As the Conservator gains experience, he or she may move up to supervise other conservators or to manage a department of conservation for an institute or a business.

Education

The educational requirements for this career are extensive and specific. The aspiring Conservator should work for a bachelor's degree in art history and a master's degree in art history or art conservation. In addition, there are specialized training schools that offer programs in restoration and conservation; such training is a must. Electives should be used to gain a full knowledge of physics and chemistry, up to the level of organic chemistry, in order to understand the science of art materials.

Experience and Skills

The art conservation training programs offer the student the kind of apprenticeship necessary for this special field. Any kind of experience working with or for a Conservator will be equally valuable.

The aspiring Conservator should have drawing and painting skills, as well as eye training to see into and beyond the surface of the artwork he or she seeks to restore.

Organizations and Associations

The professional organization for Conservators and restorers is the American Institute for Conservation of Historic and Artistic Works (see Appendix IV).

Tips for Entry

Focusing on the new and growing areas of this field, such as photograph restoration or lithograph restoration, may provide the widest possible opportunity for finding employment.

ILLUSTRATOR

CAREER PROFILE

Duties: Provide illustrations for magazines, ad agencies, publishers, etc.

Alternate Titles: None

Salary Range: $12,000 to $35,000

Employment Prospects: Good

Advancement Prospects: Poor

Prerequisites:

Education—Bachelor's degree in fine arts or diploma from an accredited art school

Experience—Work on school publications or as an assistant in a large art department

Special Skills—Wide range of art skills; communications skills; attention to detail; deadline orientation

CAREER LADDER

```
┌─────────────────────────────┐
│                             │
│        Art Director         │
│                             │
└─────────────────────────────┘

┌─────────────────────────────┐
│                             │
│         Illustrator         │
│                             │
└─────────────────────────────┘

┌─────────────────────────────┐
│      Design Assistant       │
│             or              │
│          Student            │
└─────────────────────────────┘
```

Position Description

An Illustrator's job falls between that of a commercial artist and that of an independent artist, in terms of creative freedom and control of his or her work. Like a commercial artist, an Illustrator is given guidelines and specifications by an art director as to what the finished work should be, but the nature of the work assignments tends to leave more room for creativity to the individual artist.

Illustrators work for various types of firms, often on a free-lance basis. Some of the main outlets for illustration are magazines, publishing houses and advertising agencies.

Magazine illustration involves the creation of appropriate illustrations and designs for magazine publication. Though illustration implies a Norman Rockwell type of realistic art, today's Illustrators tend to be design-oriented, using the latest computer resources to keep the look of their work current.

Publishers use Illustrators for all kinds of projects, including technical and medical illustration for textbooks and scholarly works. Medical illustration is particularly specialized, with just a few schools offering a tailor-made program for this field. Technical illustration covers a wider variety of subjects; a technical illustrator would be knowledgeable in such areas as science, mapmaking, biological subjects, geology, machinery and the solar system.

Sketch artists are Illustrators who make quick sketches and renderings for advertising agency storyboards. This is not finished artwork but a kind of first draft for a print or live-action advertisement. Much sketching work is let out on a free-lance basis; agencies also have in-house sketch artists.

Salaries

Salaries for Illustrators can range from $12,000 to $35,000. Naturally, those with more experience, or who work for larger firms, command the higher salaries. Free-lance illustrators' incomes are determined by the amount of work they take on.

Employment Prospects

Employment is fairly easy to find for a well-prepared Illustrator. There are many specialty magazines on the market today, most of which use Illustrators. The demand for Illustrators in publishing and advertising is constant, if not growing. For those who are able to work on a free-lance basis, such work can be used to gain entry to an in-house position or to supplement the income from a full-time job.

Advancement Prospects

It is difficult to advance in this career. Most Illustrators view illustration as their ultimate career goal. The next step up the ladder is art direction; such jobs are few and difficult to find, and require substantial additional experience in graphics. Advertising probably provides the best opportunity for an Illustrator to work up to an art director's spot.

Education

Illustrators should hold bachelor's degrees in fine arts or should have graduated from accredited schools of art. Master's degrees are not especially important for aspiring Illustrators, though specialized schooling—such as in medical illustration—is crucial in certain areas of the field.

Experience and Skills

Work experience as a production or design assistant in a large art department is ideal for those wishing to become Illustrators. In addition, any experience working on school publications will be valuable.

Naturally, Illustrators are expected to have well-developed art skills. Familiarity with computer graphics can be helpful. For both free-lance and in-house artists, communications skills are important in the understanding and execution of assignments. Detail orientation can be critical, especially in fields such as technical and medical illustration. Illustrators should also be able to cope with firm deadlines.

Organizations and Associations

The Society of Illustrators (see Appendix IV) is the association for members of this field. The Society publishes books and mounts exhibits of Illustrators' work.

Tips for Entry

It is important for an aspiring Illustrator to have a neat, professional-looking portfolio of work to show to potential employers. College or art school programs will enable students to prepare such portfolios; the more attention and care the student devotes to portfolio preparation, the better his or her chances for a fair hearing with a potential employer.

FINE ARTIST

Duties: Create and sell artwork

Alternate Title: Artist

Salary Range: $0 to $1,000,000

Employment Prospects: Poor

Advancement Prospects: Poor

Prequisites:

Education—None required; most have attended art school

Experience—None required

Special Skills—Art skills, creativity, talent, a good "eye," sales skills

```
┌─────────────────────────┐
│                         │
│       Fine Artist       │
│                         │
└─────────────────────────┘

┌─────────────────────────┐
│                         │
│        Student          │
│                         │
└─────────────────────────┘
```

Position Description

The job of an Artist is to create and sell artwork. Of course, many people pursue art as a hobby and do not worry about selling their work; but for those who want careers as artists, selling the work can be as important as creating it.

Artists may work in many media—painting, drawing, sculpture, printmaking, and so on—or only in one. The Artist essentially works alone, making all the decisions about the form the work is to take and the message it is to convey.

If one hopes to make a living as an Artist, it is important to be concerned with the marketing of the finished work. This can entail making sales calls on galleries, trying to find an agent or representative, or selling work on street corners and at art fairs.

Because it is difficult to make a living as a fine artist, many Artists supplement their income with other jobs. An Artist may take on free-lance illustration work or teach in an art school; he or she may go to work as a sales clerk or a secretary.

Salaries

Artists do not receive salaries as such, because they are self-employed. Artists' incomes can vary widely; most Artists make no income from their work, but some renowned Artists can earn millions of dollars.

Employment Prospects

It is difficult to make a living as an Artist. Most Artists are unable to support themselves with sales of their artwork alone.

Advancement Prospects

It is the rare Artist who is able to make a comfortable living from sales of his or her work.

Education

There are no educational requirements to become an Artist, but most Artists train in an art school, a college art department, or with private teachers.

Experience and Skills

The Artist needs experience in creating artwork and in developing contacts to sell artwork. Artists should have excellent art skills, creative ability, a good "eye," talent and sales ability.

Organizations/Associations

There are several national organizations for Artists (see Appendix IV); in addition, Artists should take advantage of the resources of their local and regional art associations.

Tips for Entry

Self-promotion is the key to making a living as an Artist. It is important to cultivate contacts with agents, galleries, museums and art dealers and collectors.

SECTION 2
MUSEUMS

INTERN

Duties: Provide research as a clerical assistant for a museum professional

Alternate Title: Volunteer

Salary Range: $0 to $13,000

Employment Prospects: Fair to good

Advancement Prospects: Fair to poor

Prerequisites:

Education—Coursework in art history or undergraduate degree

Experience—Research and clerical skills

Special Skills—Flexibility; good knowledge of an area of the museum's concentration

```
┌─────────────────────────────┐
│                             │
│     Curatorial Assistant    │
│                             │
└─────────────────────────────┘

┌─────────────────────────────┐
│                             │
│            Intern           │
│                             │
└─────────────────────────────┘

┌─────────────────────────────┐
│                             │
│           College           │
│                             │
└─────────────────────────────┘
```

Position Description

It is very difficult to obtain positions in museums, but one way to prepare oneself is through an internship. An Intern's experience varies widely from museum to museum. In some situations, he or she may be little more than an unpaid volunteer who is asked to do clerical jobs like filing and typing. Larger museums, however, often offer professional internships which carry a stipend and offer significant responsibility for a special project. In virtually every instance, an internship is valuable for someone seriously contemplating museum work, if only for the chance to observe the dynamic of the museum firsthand.

A professional-level internship in a large museum is typically highly structured. In many programs internships begin with a period of orientation in which participants observe the different departments of the institution in order to gain an impression of the overall structure of the museum. The experience of speaking with several museum professionals—in the areas of development, financial management, education, public relations and curatorial work—is itself a valuable way to gauge one's interest and aptitude in different areas of museum work. This introductory period is followed by six months or a year of work within a particular department, under the close supervision of a museum professional. Although internships are available in virtually every area of museum work, the most popular fall in the areas of education and the curatorial departments. Development, membership and public relations are also in great need of clerical and research help and often provide useful experience for those interested in the managerial end of museum work.

The particular tasks an Intern is given vary widely. In some cases, Interns are expected to do all of the miscellaneous drudgery associated with a particular department. In others, highly educated Interns may perform crucial research for a particular exhibition or even, in some cases, organize a special project on their own. However an internship is composed, it allows a participant close contact with a museum professional who can both impart knowledge and prove a useful professional contact in the future.

In addition an Intern may:

- help with museum installations
- give gallery talks or provide other basic educational services
- be required to prepare a term paper on his or her experience if the internship is associated with a degree-granting program

Salaries

Internship stipends vary greatly, though they are inevitably quite low. An Intern may be expected to work without pay. Summer internships may offer a stipend of $1,000 or $1,500, and yearlong positions could carry a salary of $10,000 to $13,000.

Employment Prospects

Even though they pay little, or nothing at all, museum internships can be surprisingly difficult to obtain. Especially in a prestigious program with real responsibilities or educational potential, getting a museum internship may be as difficult as getting a full-time museum position. However, in some museums, especially smaller ones in need of basic assistance and without the capacity to give stipends, it is often possible to gain some kind of volunteer position. In any case, the internships are open to students or recent graduates, so they offer a foot in the door of museum work without requiring previous experience.

Advancement Prospects

If an Intern does outstanding work it is often possible that he or she will be offered an entry-level job in the department the Intern worked in. Internships are an important way to make professional contacts in the small and closed world of museum work, so even if the ex-

perience does not immediately lead to a full-time job, it will probably pay off in the future.

Education

Internships with minimal responsibility can require as little as a few semesters of coursework in art history, related to one of the museum's areas of specialization. In a more structured or prestigious program, a distinguished undergraduate record is preferable, as well as special skills like writing ability or profound knowledge of a particular area of art history.

Experience and Skills

The most important thing an Intern must have is the willingness to undertake boring jobs in order to learn about museum work. This means he or she must have a sincere interest in the field and a commitment to learning about it. Most Interns do a lot of detail-oriented work, so they must be thorough and organized. They must have excellent research skills and good writing ability. Since internships can often seem loosely structured, and supervisors might be too busy to spend a lot of time with them, Interns must be able to structure their own time, and use to best advantage their chance to see the working of the museum.

CURATORIAL ASSISTANT

CAREER PROFILE

Duties: Provide secretarial and research support to curators

Alternate Title: Curatorial Secretary

Employment Prospects: Fair

Advancement Prospects: Fair to good

Prerequisites:
   Education—Undergraduate degree in art history

   Experience—Familiarity with museums and secretarial skills helpful

   Special Skills—Research ability, resourcefulness and good organizational abilities

CAREER LADDER

```
┌─────────────────────────────┐
│                             │
│      Assistant Curator      │
│                             │
└─────────────────────────────┘

┌─────────────────────────────┐
│                             │
│     Curatorial Assistant    │
│                             │
└─────────────────────────────┘

┌─────────────────────────────┐
│                             │
│    College or Internship    │
│                             │
└─────────────────────────────┘
```

Position Description

Curatorial departments generate a great deal of paperwork, including general correspondence, the compilation of accurate lists of art objects to be included in a temporary exhibition, or the preparation of loan agreement forms which are used when borrowing or lending works of art. Most curatorial departments regularly publish informational brochures, catalogues and other publications which must be typed and proofread. Record-keeping is especially important when working with art objects in transit. Curatorial Assistants provide secretarial, clerical and research support for curators in all of these areas. Usually, people who take these jobs are interested in pursuing a career in museums and bring with them a background in art.

Museums follow standard procedures to keep track of objects in their collections or works they will borrow for a temporary exhibition. Curatorial Assistants must learn these conventional methods and make sure they are followed in all of the correspondence, contracts and manuscripts generated in their department. Since most curatorial departments are understaffed, the Curatorial Assistant often becomes a jack-of-all-trades who may write letters for a curator one day and spend the next in the library researching the history of a particular painting or sculpture.

In a large museum Curatorial Assistants may be hired to work exclusively on a special project, like a major temporary exhibition. In addition to managing correspondence and basic research, the Curatorial Assistant may have important organizational duties. For instance, in a juried exhibition to which artists submit slides, the Curatorial Assistant might log in all submissions, transfer the slides to projectors for viewing and notify artists of the curator's decisions.

A Curatorial Assistant must work quickly but accurately. Mistakes can be embarrassing to the museum or detrimental to an artist, so attention to detail and the ability to meet deadlines are important attributes.

In addition a Curatorial Assistant may:
* research the location of photographs to be used in publications
* take minutes in curatorial meetings
* process bills and requests for payment in the curatorial department
* engage the museum photographer or a freelance photographer to document exhibitions

Salaries

Salaries for Curatorial Assistants tend to be quite low, ranging from $9,000 to $15,000.

Employment Prospects

The Curatorial Assistant is an entry-level job in the curatorial department and is therefore desirable in spite of its considerable secretarial and clerical duties. Although it is often difficult to get these positions, turnover is higher than in other curatorial jobs, creating more frequent openings. The applicant should have both a good general knowledge of art history and excellent secretarial skills.

Advancement Prospects

Without going back to school for a graduate degree it is difficult to advance from Curatorial Assistant to assistant curator. Chances are better for Curatorial Assistants who have worked on special projects and proven their insight and effectiveness in this context. However, Curatorial Assistants are certainly in a good position to learn the rudiments of museum work and to absorb a good deal of art history from the curators they work for.

Education

An undergraduate degree in art history or a related field is required, along with secretarial training. Proficiency with a computer is helpful.

Experience and Skills

Curatorial Assistants must be efficient and highly organized people. They must have excellent secretarial skills, including typing, filing and the ability to write basic correspondence. In addition to these practical skills, they must have a good basic knowledge of, or sensitivity to, art objects they are working with, and a disposition which can withstand pressure.

ASSISTANT CURATOR

CAREER PROFILE

Duties: Assume responsibility for one cluster of curatorial duties within a curatorial department, for instance the management of a sub-collection

Salary Range: $15,000 to $30,000

Employment Prospects: Poor to fair

Advancement Prospects: Good

Prerequisites:

Education—Undergraduate degree, and preferably an advanced degree in art history

Experience—Background in curatorial work

Special Skills—Outstanding knowledge of art history; writing skills; familiarity with collection management and the organization of special exhibitions

CAREER LADDER

```
┌─────────────────────────────────┐
│                                 │
│       Associate Curator         │
│                                 │
└─────────────────────────────────┘

┌─────────────────────────────────┐
│                                 │
│       Assistant Curator         │
│                                 │
└─────────────────────────────────┘

┌─────────────────────────────────┐
│                                 │
│      Curatorial Assistant       │
│                                 │
└─────────────────────────────────┘
```

Position Description

Although Assistant Curators are the most junior curators in a museum, they often have considerable responsibility. Like associate curators, they may be assigned to long-term projects or assume responsibility for a special sub-collection. Since there are, typically, few full curators in a museum, and only a slightly larger number of associate curators, all of whom tend to be stable in their positions, Assistant Curators may be given greater and greater responsibility in the course of their tenure at a museum but not receive a change in title.

In addition to special projects like the organization of a temporary exhibition, Assistant Curators are usually given specific research or administration-oriented duties by a senior curator. For instance, in preparation for a temporary exhibition an Assistant Curator might be asked to research the location of particular works of art, compile bibliographies on exhibiting artists, or describe specific objects to be used as catalogue entries in a publication accompanying the exhibition. Assistant Curators might take responsibility for ongoing duties, like visiting local artists to critique their work or handling general correspondence within the department.

An Assistant Curator who works closely with a particular collection may handle all administrative details relating to loan requests. Any museum with a collection receives requests from outside museums to borrow works of art for temporary exhibition. In a large museum, or one with a particularly important collection, these requests can be frequent and time-consuming. An Assistant Curator would consult with the conservator about the fitness of the work to travel, as well as with senior curators who have jurisdiction over the collection. Once a decision has been made the Assistant Curator would handle all correspondence with the outside organization, dealing with conditions of the loan or the reasons for its denial.

In a small museum, Assistant Curators' responsibilities might include secretarial support for other curators and additional clerical or organizational duties. Although many Assistant Curators are able to organize exhibitions and write about art, their jobs tend to be task-oriented and not directly related to the overall planning issues of the curatorial department.

In addition an Assistant Curator may:

- compile and coordinate the production of scholarly catalogues
- give gallery talks for the general public
- act as a liaison with the public relations officer

Salaries

Although Assistant Curators' salaries range from $15,000 to $25,000, they may be as high as $30,000 in a major museum.

Employment Prospects

As with all curatorial positions, it is very difficult to get a job as an Assistant Curator. Although in a small museum the job may be an entry-level position, this does not reduce the competition, since there are many more interested applicants than there are opportunities. It is easier to find a curatorial job in a smaller institution, but even in such museums the candidate must have distinguised him- or herself academically or with work in the field. In a large museum, Assistant Curatorships with significant responsibility are extremely difficult to get.

Advancement Prospects

Once one has entered curatorial work, chances are usually good that further opportunities will present themselves. However, it is often difficult to jump from Assistant to Associate Curator, not only because there are fewer positions as one climbs the ladder, but also because an Assistant Curatorship may not call for the creative work with which to distinguish oneself.

Education

Although an undergraduate degree in art history may be sufficient in some museums, a graduate degree in the field is necessary for an Assistant Curatorship in a large or prestigious museum.

Experience and Skills

An Assistant Curator must have an excellent grasp of art history, particularly of a specialized field relevant to the museum. He or she must have superior writing, research and public speaking skills. In a large institution it is also necessary for the Assistant Curator to be aware of the workings of a museum, including the procedure for processing loan requests and the organization of temporary exhibitions. More than senior curators, it is important that an Assistant Curator has excellent organizational skills.

ASSOCIATE CURATOR

CAREER PROFILE

CAREER LADDER

Duties: Assume responsibility for several clusters of curatorial duties within a curatorial department

Salary Range: $15,000 to $56,000

Employment Prospects: Poor to fair

Advancement Prospects: Good

Prerequisites:

Education—An undergraduate and advanced degree in art history

Experience—Considerable curatorial background, including experience in organizing exhibitions and managing collections

Special Skills—Excellent knowledge of a specialized area of art history, excellent writing skills

```
┌──────────────────────────────┐
│                              │
│          Curator             │
│                              │
└──────────────────────────────┘

┌──────────────────────────────┐
│                              │
│      Associate Curator       │
│                              │
└──────────────────────────────┘

┌──────────────────────────────┐
│                              │
│      Assistant Curator       │
│                              │
└──────────────────────────────┘
```

Position Description

The Associate Curator works in conjunction with the curator in managing a museum's collections and organizing temporary exhibitions. Although the Associate Curator has less administrative responsibility than the chief curator or curator, he or she has significant authority in developing the museum's artistic program. Although the structures of curatorial departments vary from institution to institution, it is typical for Associate Curators to deal with a broad area of the museum's program, and with the various curatorial duties which relate to that area. For instance, in a Department of Prints and Drawings, an Associate Curator might be responsible for all activities relating to drawings, including the acquisition of works as well as the organization of temporary exhibitions. A department may be structured so that an Associate Curator supervises all temporary exhibitions within it; in some museums, an Associate Curator is responsible for all research related to works in the collection.

Regardless of what the Associate Curator's specific responsibilities are, the job is usually structured so that he or she spends the preponderance of the time planning and implementing a limited number of projects from start to finish. For instance, in a large museum with an active Department of Painting and Sculpture, an Associate Curator may spend two or three years working intensively on a single major exhibition, researching works of art relevant to a theme, undertaking correspondence with potential lenders of art, preparing a catalogue, and communicating the goals and themes of the exhibition to other members of the staff, like the curator for education, the public relations officer and the grants officer. The Associate Curator may be responsible for supervising the growth, maintenance and interpretation of a particular aspect of the collection. For instance, within the area of ancient art, he or she might be responsible for Egyptian artifacts.

In addition to responsibilities related to his or her own projects, Associate Curators may share some of the Curator's administrative responsibilities. He or she may supervise an assistant curator or have a fund-raising responsibility related to specific exhibitions or collections. In many museums, certain exhibitions or programs are developed collaboratively among a group of Associate Curators.

In addition the Associate Curator may:

- manage an administrative area of curatorial activity, like the request of loans from the permanent collection
- consult with the chief curator and curator in long-range planning for the department
- contribute articles to museum publications

Salaries

The salary for Associate Curators ranges from $15,000 to $56,000, but averages somewhere in the area of $15,000 to $25,000.

Employment Prospects

As with all curatorial positions, it is very difficult to get a job as an Associate Curator. It is possible to enter this position right after receiving an advanced degree in art history, but chances are better if the candidate has had three to five years of curatorial experience.

Advancement Prospects

In most museums Associate Curator is a mid-level or senior position, with a lot of room to prove him or herself through publications, the building of collections and the organization of exhibitions. Prospects are therefore good that an Associate Curator will advance to the position of curator and eventually chief curator. In most institutions, and especially in larger, prestigious museums, curators hold their positions for many years, so the prospects are often better for advancement if one looks outside of one's present institution.

Education

An undergraduate degree in art history or a related field is required, and usually an advanced degree in art history is necessary.

Experience and Skills

The Associate Curator must be able to manage a project well from start to finish. This involves excellent planning skills, the ability to communicate a project's goals and to research funding, as well as an excellent knowledge of art history and superior writing and communication skills. The Associate Curator must be aware of the procedural and legal aspects of museum collections, as well as the methods utilized in researching and seeking art objects for a temporary exhibition. He or she must be able to stay abreast of new art-historical attitudes and insights into his or her field, and combine intellectual flexibility and curiosity with administrative skills.

CURATOR

Duties: Supervision of activity and personnel in a major set of curatorial programs, or of a curatorial department

Salary Range: $26,000 to $80,000+

Employment Prospects: Poor to fair

Advancement Prospects: Good

Prerequisites:

Education—Undergraduate and advanced degrees in art history

Experience—Extensive curatorial background, distinguished contribution to his or her field of art history

Special Skills—Excellent writing skills, creativity in art-historical point of view, and excellent ability to interpret works of art

Chief Curator

Curator

Associate Curator

Position Description

Under the supervision of the chief curator are a group of Curators who are responsible for a major constellation of activities or departments of the museum—e.g. the department of antiquities or of twentieth century painting and sculpture. Each Curator has administrative duties related to his or her area of specialization, and has primary responsibility for exhibitions, research, publications, acquisitions and donor contracts within this area. The Curator may also supervise other associate and assistant curators on his or her curatorial team. In a small museum the positions of Curator and chief curator may be combined, and there may be greater flexibility in the division of responsibility within a curatorial department.

The Curator of a collection in a museum has two broad objectives: to build a comprehensive collection of high quality within his or her area and to interpret this collection through publications and special exhibitions. Curators must spend a good deal of their time researching and acquiring objects for the collection. This means attending international auctions as well as cultivating relationships with major private collectors, in the hope that they will eventually leave their collections to the museum. Building a fine museum collection requires a master of the art history for the period of the collection as well as the subtle ability to represent the depth and richness of a historical period or an artist through a limited number of objects. Every Curator has a different amount of acquisition funds available to him or her, and each must deal with the relative scarcity of art objects, but all must be able to work within these limitations to create a collection of quality and historical importance.

Not only must the Curator put together museum collections, but he or she must also interpret them for the public. This includes the installation of the collection in the museum's galleries in such a way as to indicate an historical progression; the publication of catalogues which describe the significance of particular objects in the collection; or the organization of special exhibitions which explore in depth an aspect of the collection. Often, the temporary exhibition of a private collector's works is a means of attracting a gift from that collection in the future.

When organizing a temporary exhibition the Curator must develop the exhibition's theme and compile a list of artists to be included. He or she, with the help of associate and assistant curators, must then research the availability of objects and request to borrow them from other institutions, individuals or galleries. Most temporary exhibitions are accompanied by interpretive catalogues written or edited by the Curator. When outside institutions make requests to borrow objects in the museum's collection, the Curator, in conjunction with junior members of the staff, the registrar and the conservator, determines whether the loan should be made.

Although most Curators spend the preponderance of their time working with art, they also share responsibility with the department of development for raising money for their programs, and have the administrative responsibility for managing budgets and personnel relevant to their activity.

In addition a Curator may:
• lecture to the public on the museum's collections
• contribute articles to scholarly art journals on objects in the museum's collection
• provide advice for private collectors associated with the museum
• authenticate objects within his or her area of specialization

Salaries

Curators average a salary between $26,000 and $40,000, though the average is higher in larger museums and may be as high as $80,000.

Employment Prospects

Positions as Curator are extremely difficult to get and require proven expertise in an area of specialization as well as an impressive record of publications and exhibitions. The Curator in many museums is as much a scholar as an administrator, so the necessary qualifications for the job are often as rigorous as those for a college professor.

Advancement Prospects

Advancement prospects for the Curator are very good. He or she may advance to the position of chief curator and eventually director if performance has been impressive.

Education

The Curator should have an undergraduate degree in art history and a graduate degree in his or her area of specialization. As with the chief curator, a graduate degree is not always absolutely necessary, but it is a great advantage.

Experience and Skills

The Curator must have expertise in his or her area of specialization as well as excellent writing, research and public speaking skills. He or she must be familiar with the conservation principles of art objects, as well as know the current market, collecting ethics and customs regulations in the area of specialization. Good Curators have a special affinity for, and sensitivity to, art objects which is hard to describe or quantify. In addition the Curator must be an efficieint administrator and be able to research and request funds from private and public sources. Since most Curators work closely with private collectors, they must have a skillful and subtle facility for social interaction.

CHIEF CURATOR

Duties: Supervise artistic direction and administration of all curatorial departments

Salary Range: $30,000 to $70,000 +

Employment Prospects: Poor to fair

Advancement Prospects: Good

Prerequisites:
  Education—Undergraduate and advanced degree in art history

  Experience—Extensive curatorial background and administrative skills

  Special Skills—Excellent scholarly and creative grasp of art history; administrative, planning and leadership ability

```
┌─────────────────────────┐
│                         │
│        Director         │
│                         │
└─────────────────────────┘

┌─────────────────────────┐
│                         │
│      Chief Curator      │
│                         │
└─────────────────────────┘

┌─────────────────────────┐
│                         │
│        Curator          │
│                         │
└─────────────────────────┘
```

Position Description

The Chief Curator is one of the key positions in a museum. He or she has administrative responsibility for curatorial affairs and, in cooperation with the director, outlines the museum's curatorial policy. The Chief Curator supervises the creation and growth of collections as well as the museum's development of temporary exhibitions. This job includes considerable fund-raising and contact with benefactors, as well as responsibility for developing a budget for the curatorial department and supervision of its staff. In addition to these administrative responsibilities, the Chief Curator also organizes exhibitions and acquires and interprets objects in his or her area of specialization.

Curators are responsible for both the acquisition and care of museum collections and the organization of temporary exhibitions. In some institutions these different duties are shared equally by a group of curators; in others, curators specialize in temporary exhibitions while their colleagues are entirely concerned with the care of a particular segment of the collection. The Chief Curator must structure this activity in a way appropriate to the areas of interest of the institution. He or she develops an exhibition policy which responds to the needs of the community, the strengths of the museum and its staff, and activity in the field at large.

The Chief Curator and the director are the primary spokespeople to the community for the museum's collections and exhibitions. They must communicate the goals and activities of the curatorial departments to potential funders in the public and private sectors as well as to volunteer groups which help to fund the museum. The Chief Curator seeks and maintains contacts with collectors and benefactors in the community with the hope that they will contribute money or works of art to the institution.

Although the Chief Curator may not be directly involved in the daily work of maintaining a collection or organizing exhibitions, he or she is intimately involved with all major artistic decisions made by members of the department. Especially in large museums with encyclopedic collections ranging from ancient objects to contemporary art, the Chief Curator must balance the activities of the various departments and work toward an integrated program. The Chief Curator also communicates curatorial needs and directions to the director of finance, the director of development, the curator for education, and often the public relations officer.

In addition the Chief Curator may:
- supervise museum publications
- develop a fund-raising strategy for the curatorial department

Salaries

Chief Curators average salaries between $30,000 and $40,000. Salaries are directly related to the size of a museum and can be as high as $70,000 in a major institution with a great deal of curatorial activity.

Employment Prospects

The position of Chief Curator is one of the most highly sought-after jobs in museum work, and competition is extremely stiff. At all but the smallest museums, an applicant must have built a significant reputation in the field before he or she is able to reach this position.

Advancement Prospects

As in all curatorial work, one's record of exhibitions and publications is a primary test of ability. With a good reputation as a curator, as well as proven effectiveness as an administrator, prospects are good for a Chief Curator to advance to the position of director at his or her own institution or another museum.

Education

In virtually every case an undergraduate degree in art history or a related field and a graduate degree in art history, with a concentration in one of the areas of interest of the museum, are necessary. It is often possible, especially in institutions which collect and exhibit only contemporary art, to attain the position of Chief Curator without a graduate degree, but in this case an impressive record of publications and exhibitions is necessary.

Experience and Skills

Not only must the Chief Curator have demonstrated a high level of ability in interpreting works of art, organizing exhibitions, and building collections, but he or she must also be an effective administrator, able to manage a large budget and raise funds in the community. An excellent grasp of art history and superior writing and communications skills are necessary, as well as a flair for diplomacy. The Chief Curator must be adept at planning and be able to take into account issues of marketing and development when designing exhibition policy. The ability to manage a staff is necessary, as well as a proficiency in working with department heads of other areas of the museum.

GUARD

Duties: Ensure the safety of art objects in the museum's galleries

Salary Range: $8 to $9 an hour

Employment Prospects: Fair to good

Advancement Prospects: Poor

Prerequisites:
  Education— High school-level education

  Experience— None

  Special Skills— Responsibility and reliability

```
┌─────────────────────────────┐
│      Guard Supervisor       │
└─────────────────────────────┘

┌─────────────────────────────┐
│            Guard            │
└─────────────────────────────┘

┌─────────────────────────────┐
│   High School or College    │
└─────────────────────────────┘
```

Position Description

Although museum Guards may have a variety of responsibilities, their basic duty is to ensure the safety of works of art in the museum's galleries. Often the position is narrowly defined and Guards are asked only to patrol their assigned area within the museum, making sure that visitors do not touch or otherwise damage art objects. In smaller museums, however, Guards may be asked to help out in a number of ways. In some cases they may be trained to discuss the works of art with visitors; they may assist in the maintenance of the building by vacuuming or otherwise cleaning the galleries; or they may participate in the installation of exhibitions.

Works of art are often extremely fragile and in peril from even minimal contact with the human hand. Guards must be extremely vigilant in observing the activities of museum visitors—especially when the galleries are crowded. In a large museum Guards are an important source of information: They are often asked where a particular exhibition or work of art is located. Although ostensibly passive, Guards are often called upon to give information about museum programs and services. In smaller museums they may participate in special training programs which prepare them to discuss works of art as well as provide information.

Guards report to a guard supervisor who in turn reports either to the director of finance or to another museum professional in charge of the operation of the building. Because the safety of the museum's collection lies greatly in their hands, Guards are expected to be conscientious, punctual and well-disciplined. Often they are given some training in conservation issues in order to recognize damage to an art object. When special events occur in a small museum—like openings, lectures or performances—Guards are asked to help control crowds and set up special equipment.

Although museum guarding is not an exciting job, or one with much potential for professional growth, it does provide a glimpse into the workings of a museum which might prove valuable for art or art history students.

In addition a Guard might:
• run errands for museum staff when galleries are closed
• be responsible for activating electronic surveillance systems or alarm systems

Salaries

Salaries range from minimum wage to $8 or $9 per hour. For a long-time employee this wage might be higher.

Employment Prospects

Since very few specific skills are needed to become a Guard, it can be a very easy way of entering a museum. In larger museums, the Guards might have a union organization, and in smaller operations, flexibility and special skills like carpentry or knowledge of history might be a benefit.

Advancement Prospects

Aside from advancing to the position of guard supervisor, there is little chance of advancement from this position in all but the smallest museums. In such institutions, a Guard with talents or training in art history might be offered an entry-level job.

Education

No specific education is necessary, although any training in art or art history, or knowledge of carpentry or conservation procedures, may be seen as an advantage.

Experience and Skills

The most important quality for a museum Guard is reliability. It is of the utmost importance that he or she reports to work on time and is thorough and vigilant in supervising the galleries. In a small museum, where Guards might be called upon for any number of purposes, training in art history or art, or carpentry skills, is important. A Guard's disposition should be pleasant and polite since he or she is one of the most visible representatives of the museum for visitors. It is preferable that the guard take an interest in the museum's programs so as to be able to explain them to visitors and direct them to an appropriate gallery or event when necessary.

GUARD SUPERVISOR

CAREER PROFILE

Duties: Manage museum guard staff

Salary Range: $15,000 to $25,000

Employment Prospects: Fair

Advancement Prospects: Poor to fair

Prerequisites:
   Education—Undergraduate degree in business or museum studies

   Experience—Background in personnel management, art conservation

   Special Skills—Excellent organizational ability, good interpersonal skills

CAREER LADDER

```
┌─────────────────────────────┐
│                             │
│     Director of Finance     │
│                             │
└─────────────────────────────┘

┌─────────────────────────────┐
│                             │
│      Guard Supervisor       │
│                             │
└─────────────────────────────┘

┌─────────────────────────────┐
│                             │
│            Guard            │
│                             │
└─────────────────────────────┘
```

Position Description

The Guard Supervisor is responsible for hiring, firing, evaluating and scheduling the museum's guards. He or she is responsible to the director of finance, and must have excellent organizational and interpersonal skills. With the director of finance the Guard Supervisor either helps plan or simply implements personnel policy for the guards as well as scheduling working shifts for them.

The Guard Supervisor is the primary liaison between the museum staff and the gallery personnel. An important part of this job involves communicating the museum's policies and programs to the guards. He or she must be totally aware of the methods of employee evaluation, the salary structure and the special benefits of the guard staff, and must be available to discuss these issues with those under his or her supervision. It is important that the person in this position stay aware of museum programs and policies and also create a mechanism for making the guards aware of them, through either regular meetings or printed notices.

The Guard Supervisor must master the museum's electronic or other security systems and be proficient in their operation. He or she is responsible for deactivating these systems when the museum opens in the morning, and turning them on when it closes at night. The Guard Supervisor must work closely with the museum personnel who plan special events in order to provide necessary guard services or extra manpower when needed.

Guards are a central part of the museum's security so it is extremely important that the Guard Supervisor be aware of the performance of his or her employees. He or she must frequently survey the galleries and often provide written reports on the guards. Turnover can be high among guards so the Guard Supervisor must be aware of methods of recruiting new employees through advertising or a network of contacts, and be able to effectively assess the qualifications of an applicant through an interview and reference checks.

The Guard Supervisor must be a versatile, trustworthy person who is able to handle a great deal of administrative detail, from scheduling several employees to communicating to them their benefits—and must also possess leadership qualities.

In addition the Guard Supervisor may:

- plan and schedule educational seminars for the guards
- assist in museum installations or preparations for special events, especially in a small museum
- assist in building maintenance

Employment Prospects

Employment prospects are fair for the position of Guard Supervisor. Since this person is relied upon to maintain an important aspect of museum security, experience in a security-related or administrative position, with impeccable references, is necessary. It is possible that an outstanding guard could achieve this position in a smaller museum. In a larger museum managerial experience, particularly in a personnel-related area, would be desirable.

Salary

Depending upon the number of guards under their supervision Guard Supervisors can make between $15,000 and $25,000 and sometimes more.

Advancement Prospects

Advancement prospects for the Guard Supervisor are not too good as a rule, but in a large museum it may be possible for the Guard Supervisor to be promoted to a position of greater authority in the finance department.

Education

Training in management, particularly with regard to personnel, is desirable. Training in art history can be an advantage, especially when there is a special guard training program in the museum. Some formal acquaintance with security systems would be an advantage.

Experience and Skills

The most important skill a Guard Supervisor must possess is excellent organizational ability. He or she must manage a complex set of schedules as well as salary and program information. Flexibility and a good rapport with people are necessary, since the Guard Supervisor must bridge the gap which often exists between the museum's professional staff and the guards. Knowledge of art history, conservation principles and the ability to handle works of art are all advantageous.

PUBLIC RELATIONS ASSISTANT

CAREER PROFILE

Duties: Manage the clerical activity of the public relations department and assist in preparing press materials

Salary Range: $10,000 to $17,000

Employment Prospects: Fair to good

Advancement Prospects: Fair to good

Prerequisites:
Education—Undergraduate degree in public relations, journalism or the liberal arts

Experience—Excellent secretarial skills

Special Skills—Knowledge of art history, familiarity with the structures and methods of servicing the press

CAREER LADDER

```
┌─────────────────────────────┐
│   Public Relations Officer   │
└─────────────────────────────┘

┌─────────────────────────────┐
│   Public Relations Assistant │
└─────────────────────────────┘

┌─────────────────────────────┐
│           College            │
└─────────────────────────────┘
```

Position Description

A great deal of information is processed and circulated by the museum's public relations department. The Public Relations Assistant is responsible for maintaining efficient systems for disseminating this information to the press and the general public. Although responsibilities include a good deal of clerical and organizational work, like typing and copying press releases, supervising mailings and maintaining a file of press clippings, the Public Relations Assistant is usually given ample opportunity to develop his or her writing skills and to work directly with members of the press.

The public relations department provides several different types of information, ranging from brief listings or copy for short public service announcements on radio and television to detailed program descriptions that are many pages long. For each of these types of press release, and for different media outlets like daily and weekly newspapers, magazines, radio and television, there are specific deadlines for information. The Public Relations Assistant must maintain an accurate schedule of deadlines so that releases are sent out on time and to the proper people. He or she supervises bulk mailings of this material and answers telephone inquiries from members of the press.

When a magazine or television station decides to do a story on an exhibition or program, they usually require materials like photographs, slides and background reading. Members of the press often like to speak to curators or artists. In advance of a program or exhibition the Public Relations Assistant works with the curatorial department and the public relations officer to identify, obtain and reproduce black and white photographs and photocopied articles that will be made available for the press. During the course of the program he or she will provide further supplementary materials to the press when necessary.

One of the most important resources the public relations department maintains is a file or scrapbook of clippings. The Public Relations Assistant is responsible for finding and compiling this material, or gathering it from a clipping service.

In addition the Public Relations Assistant may:
• assist in writing and editing the museum's newsletter
• write short releases or public service announcements
• coordinate invitations and refreshments for press conferences

Salaries

Depending upon the size of the public relations department and the writing responsibilities of the Public Relations Assistant, he or she can make between $10,000 and $17,000.

Employment Prospects

Positions as Public Relations Assistant are entry-level jobs and provide a good overall introduction to the mechanics of press relations as well as the structure of the museum. Competition is tough, but it is generally less difficult than getting an entry-level position in a curatorial department.

Advancement Prospects

Since publicizing a museum requires a sensitivity to art and a knowledge of the specialized art press, as well as competence in the basic procedures of press relations, Public Relations Assistants who learn the field by participating in it have a good chance to move up to the job of public relations officer. It is also possible that the Public Relations Assistant may be promoted to other administrative posts within the museum in fund-raising or financial management, or to an entry-level job in the curatorial department.

Education

Although a special degree in public relations, journalism or communications is not necessary, it would be helpful. Secretarial programs and proficiency on the computer are valuable training for this job. Coursework in art history and a demonstrated skill at writing are crucial.

Experience and Skills

The Public Relations Assistant must be levelheaded and very well organized. He or she must be able to coordinate as many as 30 press releases at a time and cheerfully explain programs and seek out supplementary information for members of the press. A good writer will go far in this job, as the public relations officer learns that he or she can delegate press release writing to the Assistant. Fast and accurate typing and research skills are a must.

Organizations and Associations

The Public Relations Society of America (see Appendix IV) serves public relations professionals in all types of organizations.

PUBLIC RELATIONS OFFICER

CAREER PROFILE

Duties: Communicating the goals and programs of the museum to the print and electronic press

Alternate Title: Director of Public Relations

Salary Range: $18,000 to $40,000

Employment Prospects: Poor to fair

Advancement Prospects: Fair to good

Prerequisites:

Education—Undergraduate degree in public relations, journalism or communications

Experience—Background in press relations, knowledge of the procedures of promotion and advertising

Special Skills—Excellent writing skills, interpersonal ability and knowledge of art history

CAREER LADDER

```
┌─────────────────────────────────┐
│                                 │
│       Director of Finance       │
│                                 │
└─────────────────────────────────┘

┌─────────────────────────────────┐
│                                 │
│     Public Relations Officer    │
│                                 │
└─────────────────────────────────┘

┌─────────────────────────────────┐
│                                 │
│    Public Relations Assistant   │
│                                 │
└─────────────────────────────────┘
```

Position Description

Attendance is directly related to a museum's image and its effectiveness in communicating its exhibitions and other programs to a broad public. The Public Relations Officer is responsible for developing a positive profile for the museum through press relations with newspapers, radio, television and other media. The Public Relations Officer provides the press with a variety of news releases and listings describing museum programs and exhibitions. Since a good press release often makes the difference between an exhibition that is reviewed and one that is ignored, the Public Relations Officer must be able to write concise, arresting summaries of a variety of museum programs.

Most museums publish a newsletter to make their members, patrons and the general public aware of upcoming events. In addition to schedules and exhibition descriptions the newsletter often includes general institutional news, special articles or even art-historical essays. The Public Relations Officer has editorial responsibility for this publication. He or she must work closely with the curatorial departments to collect information about upcoming programs and write about them. Since the newsletter is typically considered an important benefit for museum members, the Public Relations Officer often works closely with the membership officer to develop its format and content.

In many museums the responsibilities of the Public Relations Officer include publishing an annual report.

As the primary liaison between museum staff and the general public, the Public Relations Officer must interpret complex artistic concepts in terms that a general audience can appreciate. As in every aspect of public relations work, those entrusted with publicizing a museum do much of their work informally by getting to know, and regularly speaking with, members of the press.

In addition the Public Relations Officer may:
- organize press conferences for special events
- engage and work with an outside public relations or marketing firm
- help develop income-producing activities like catalogue distribution or bookstore management
- participate in long-range programmatic planning

Salaries

Public Relations Officers typically earn between $18,000 and $25,000, although salaries can be as high as $40,000 in a large museum in a major city. If the Public Relations Officer works primarily with national press and is involved in forging an overall marketing strategy for the museum, salaries tend to be higher.

Employment Prospects

Since working in museum public relations is attractive to writers interested in art, competition is often stiff. Writing skills and press connections provide an advantage, as does familiarity with several of the areas in which the museum has programs. In a small museum this position can be entry-level.

Advancement Prospects

Since the Public Relations Officer is usually the senior member of a small department, there is little room for growth within this area. However, his or her job responsibilities include a significant amount of marketing or strategic planning, so the Public Relations Officer might advance to fund-raising as development officer. The museum is a good training ground for publicizing a broad range of activities, and many museum Public Relations Officers advance to related jobs outside of the arts.

Education

An undergraduate degree in public relations, journalism or communications and coursework in art history are basic training for a Public Relations Officer.

Any special courses in public speaking, writing, editorial work or marketing are advantageous. Since the Public Relations Officer supervises regular mailings of press information, strong organizational and clerical skills come in handy.

Experience and Skills

It is essential that the Public Relations Officer write well and quickly. Experience as a journalist is invaluable, as is previous work in public relations. Since responsibilities include interviewing the curatorial staff for information, a knowledge of art history and an ability to sensitively encapsulate ideas are important. Deadlines are a constant reality for the Public Relations Officer, so the ability to handle pressure and react calmly is a great advantage. Since the Public Relations Officer is an important representative of the museum, he or she must speak well and skillfully initiate and maintain relationships with press people.

Organizations and Associations

The professional association for public relations officers is the Public Relations Society of America (see Appendix IV).

OFFICE MANAGER

CAREER PROFILE

Duties: Coordinate daily operations and clerical activities in a large department or the entire organization, if a small museum

Salary Range: $10,000 to $15,000 +

Employment Prospects: Fair to good

Advancement Prospects: Fair

Prerequisites:

Education—Undergraduate degree in art history preferred

Experience—Excellent secretarial skills, elementary knowledge of accounting, ability to use computers

Special Skills—Good organizational ability and interpersonal skills

CAREER LADDER

```
┌─────────────────────────┐
│                         │
│     Department Head     │
│                         │
└─────────────────────────┘

┌─────────────────────────┐
│                         │
│     Office Manager      │
│                         │
└─────────────────────────┘

┌─────────────────────────┐
│                         │
│   Department Assistant  │
│                         │
└─────────────────────────┘
```

Position Description

In a large museum major departments may have an Office Manager who coordinates daily operations. In a smaller museum the Office Manager is responsible for developing clerical and administrative systems for the entire staff. The Office Manager is an entry-level position which can be a good introduction to museum work for someone considering further education or a career in arts administration.

The Office Manager is generally supervised by the finance director and may assist with day-to-day accounting by receiving bills and sending them to the appropriate staff member to be approved and then submitting them for payment. He or she might also be responsible for accounting and dispensing petty cash to staff and ordering office supplies and furniture as necessary. Acquisition and maintenance of copy machines and computer systems are among the Office Manager's responsibilities, and he or she may also negotiate service contracts with vendors.

In a small department or museum, the Office Manager provides primary secretarial support for staff members, including typing, filing and, sometimes, program research. Most museums use volunteers or students to help with clerical work. The Office Manager coordinates and instructs these volunteers and manages special programs like work-study employment. If there are other secretaries in the department, the Office Manager supervises their work and enlists them to help with special projects.

In addition to managing the distribution of incoming mail, the Office Manager is responsible for outgoing mail, including bulk mailings, courier services and special overnight carriers. Since Office Managers can have many bosses, and many responsibilities within the museum, they must be organized, hardworking and able to withstand pressure.

In addition the Office Manager may:

- assist in the preparation of grant applications
- act as receptionist for the museum
- call staff meetings; prepare minutes and circulate them

Salaries

Office Managers make between $10,000 and $15,000. When the position includes significant administrative responsibility—for instance, managing a complex computer system—Office Managers can make higher salaries.

Employment Prospects

Turnover in this position, which is often filled by young people interested in getting a taste of museum work before going on to a better job or an advanced degree, is often very high. With excellent secretarial skills and an interest in museum work demonstrated through past internships or coursework, the prospects for getting a museum job as Office Manager are good.

Advancement Prospects

The Office Manager's prospects for advancement are only fair, and are especially limited in a large museum. In a smaller institution, an Office Manager with training in art history and a commitment to museum work can move into the position of membership officer or grants officer, or perhaps assistant to the director. People committed to a career in museum work often see the position of Office Manager as an interim step between college and further education.

Education

A degree in art history is preferred, but not necessary. A secretarial course and computer proficiency, as well as a background in accounting, are valuable.

Experience and Skills

Although Office Managers are often hired right out of college, some kind of secretarial experience is invaluable. Knowledge of elementary bookkeeping procedures and experience on computers are benefits. Experience working well with people is crucial. The Office Manager must be able to work efficiently on many things at once and be able to keep a cool head in the face of deadlines and conflicts between staff members.

REGISTRAR

CAREER PROFILE

Duties: Supervise cataloguing and maintenance of museum collections

Salary Range: $16,000 to $45,000

Employment Prospects: Poor to fair

Advancement Prospects: Fair to good

Prerequisites:

Education—Undergraduate degree in art history and training in handling artworks

Experience—Knowledge of registrarial and conservation procedures

Special Skills—Good interpersonal and administrative skills, knowledge of the technical procedures of creating and maintaining artworks

CAREER LADDER

```
┌─────────────────────────────┐
│                             │
│  Director or Chief Curator  │
│                             │
└─────────────────────────────┘

┌─────────────────────────────┐
│                             │
│         Registrar           │
│                             │
└─────────────────────────────┘

┌─────────────────────────────┐
│                             │
│     Assistant Registrar     │
│                             │
└─────────────────────────────┘
```

Position Description

The Registrar works directly with the museum's collections: He or she maintains orderly files on each work, supervises packing and shipping of incoming and outgoing loans and, with the conservator, works to ensure the artwork's proper storage and maintenance. Perhaps no one in the museum knows its collections as intimately as the Registrar, who must combine a knowledge of art history with administrative skills.

When an object enters the museum's collection it is documented by a card or file which includes the artist's full name, the exact title of the work, the materials used to make it, how it was purchased or who gave it to the museum. Along with this basic information, the Registrar typically records the provenance of the object—where it was made, who owned it and any special historical significance. A complete list of the exhibitions in which the artwork has been included as well as a summary of its condition while in the museum's collection supplement each object's file.

When the museum organizes a special exhibiton which includes art borrowed from other institutions or individuals, or when objects from the museum's collections are requested for exhibition elsewhere, the Registrar is responsible for proper packing and shipping of the artwork. This includes making arrangements for the fabrication of crates, working

with fine art shippers to schedule pickups and deliveries and preparing paperwork to document transfer of the art object. When international shipping is necessary the Registrar must handle the customs proceedings or work with a customs agent.

Often works of art are given to a museum with special stipulations or on extended loan. The Registrar must be aware of the laws concerning gifts to museums as well as those pertaining to copyrights and the right to photographically reproduce a work. The Registrar works closely with the museum's insurance agent to develop a policy which will adequately protect the collection. He or she prepares insurance claims for damaged objects. The Registrar also oversees the storage facilities for works of art in the museum, and keeps track of the location of each particular work.

The Registrar works closely with the curatorial staff to arrange shipping for temporary exhibitions and to provide information on the characteristics, history and condition of objects in the collection. Along with the conservator, the Registrar is always consulted to determine the fitness of a particular artwork to travel.

In addition the Registrar may:
- prepare a catalogue of the museum's collection
- conduct research on specific objects in the collection
- assist the curatorial staff in organizing ex-

hibitions drawn from the museum's collections
* participate in workshops on conservation techniques

Salaries

Depending on the size of the collections in his or her care, the Registrar's salary averages between $16,000 and $30,000. In a large museum a Registrar can make as much as $45,000.

Employment Prospects

The Registrar is entrusted with the care of the museum's collection, so it is unlikely that anyone without a good deal of experience in museum registration or a curatorial field would be hired. In an arts organization without a collection Registrars are often hired to oversee the shipping and handling of art. This kind of position is easier to get with minimal experience.

Advancement Prospects

The prospects for advancement depend on the Registrar's ambitions. In many smaller museums, the Registrar is also a part-time curator, and this kind of split job may lead to an entirely curatorial position. In a large museum, registrarial work is complex and satisfying. Once one has learned the field, the chances for advancement to better jobs in other museums are good.

Education

The Registrar should have a degree in art history, and particularly in the area of the museum's specialization, or some degree in the liberal arts. Coursework in library science or museum administration is valuable, as is an advanced degree or some training in conservation techniques and principles.

Experience and Skills

There is an accepted universal process for recording information about works of art which the Registrar should know well, or at least be familiar with. Previous experience in a registrarial position is invaluable, as is a knowledge of conservation and proper storage prodecures. Since a large part of the Registrar's work is administrative, he or she should be aware of the records management and data processing systems, as well as the insurace requirements for the storage and transportation of art. The Registrar must work with professionals ranging from fine arts shippers to lawyers to curators. Excellent communciations skills and a high level of organization are a great advantage.

CONSERVATOR

CAREER PROFILE

Duties: Ensure the physical safety of art objects and repair them when necessary

Salary Range: $28,000 to $55,000

Employment Prospects: Fair to good

Advancement Prospects: Good

Prerequisites:

Education—Graduate training in conservation, undergraduate degree in art history or related field

Experience—Background in the technology of art materials and conservation techniques

Special Skills—Sensitivity to art objects, good personal artistic ability

CAREER LADDER

```
┌─────────────────────────────────┐
│                                 │
│  Registrar or Director of Finance │
│                                 │
└─────────────────────────────────┘

┌─────────────────────────────────┐
│                                 │
│           Conservator           │
│                                 │
└─────────────────────────────────┘

┌─────────────────────────────────┐
│                                 │
│      Assistant Conservator      │
│                                 │
└─────────────────────────────────┘
```

Position Description

The purpose of a collecting museum is not just to purchase and exhibit works of art, but also to ensure that they are properly stored and maintained. The Conservator works closely with the registrar to prevent the deterioration of artworks, and he or she treats them when damage occurs. Conservators are as much scientists as museum professionals; they must be rigorously trained in the technology and materials originally used to make the works of art or decorative objects collected by a museum, and also trained in the chemical and physical processes of their deterioration.

The Conservator sees that objects are fumigated, kept at proper levels of humidity and protected from air pollutants or exposure to damaging light intensities and wavelengths. Depending upon what kind of objects are involved—and in a museum they could range from a delicate watercolor to an Egyptian mummy—different procedures are necessary for protection. Often a conservation department in a major museum includes specialists in several different types of objects.

In order to keep track of the condition of the museum's collections the Conservator periodically writes reports on specific objects. Whenever a request is made from an outside institution to borrow a work from the museum's collection, the Conservator is asked to examine that object and make a recommendation on its fitness to travel. The decision of the Conservator is crucial to the museum's ability to lend works. In some cases, the Conservator will specify conditions under which the object may be exhibited—for example, special levels of light or protective cases.

The conservation field has changed dramatically in the course of the 20th century in response to new technologies for cleaning and restoring a work of art as well as new philosophical attitudes toward how much an original object should be modified in order to repair it. It is crucial that the Conservator keep his or her knowledge current by belonging to a professional conservation organization which expects adherence to a code of ethics.

In addition the Conservator may:

- treat or report on objects owned by private collectors or other museums
- work closely with the curatorial staff to inform them of proper conservation procedures
- enlist the opinion of outside conservation specialists

Salaries

The average salary range for Conservators is $28,000 to $40,000. If the Conservator supervises a large department of conservation scientists, or his or her expertise is highly specialized, salaries can be as high as $55,000.

Employment Prospects

Conservation is a small field but requires extensive training and experience as well as an artistic affinity to the objects one will work on. Once the proper training is received, chances are good for employment.

Advancement Prospects

A good Conservator is crucial to the maintenance of the museum's collection. Once one has demonstrated his or her competence, prospects for advancement are very good.

Education

It is necessary for Conservators to have graduate-level training, in a conservation program of two or more years, in the theory, principles and practice of conservation, including a year's training in the principles of general material conservation and a min-imum of one year's training or internship in a special field. Undergraduate training should include courses in cultural or art history, scientific studies such as chemistry, physics or biology, studio arts and manual skills.

Experience and Skills

Most positions require at least two years of postgraduate on-the-job experience. In addition to good scientific, artistic and technical skills, the Conservator must have good writing skills and the ability to work well with the registrar and curators. Since the Conservator must maintain a laboratory, he or she must have administrative skills as well.

Organizations and Associations

The professional organization for Conservators is the American Institute for Conservation of Historic and Artistic Works (see Appendix IV).

TEACHER

Duties: Teach museum-sponsored classes for schoolchildren or adults

Alternate Title: Instructor, Lecturer

Salary Range: $10,000 to $20,000

Employment Prospects: Fair

Advancement Prospects: Fair to good

Prerequisites:
Education—Undergraduate degree in education or art history
Experience—Background in teaching art history and studio art
Special Skills—Creative grasp of art history, rapport with children

```
┌─────────────────────────────────┐
│   Head of Outreach Education    │
└─────────────────────────────────┘

┌─────────────────────────────────┐
│            Teacher              │
└─────────────────────────────────┘

┌─────────────────────────────────┐
│  College or Graduate Training   │
└─────────────────────────────────┘
```

Position Description

Teachers teach the museum's outreach education programs. There may be one or several teachers within the education department, or in a small museum the head of outreach education may do most of the teaching him- or herself. The Teacher is supervised by the head of outreach education and, although it is not the Teacher's responsibility to originate curricula for outreach seminars or other education programs, he or she usually has a good deal of impact on programs during the process of planning and development.

Museum Teachers typically work primarily with children. Three types of programs are most common: studio art classes, single visits to the museum by groups of schoolchildren, and multi-session seminars for a small number of students. In many communities a museum is an important adjunct to the school system, providing special programs in the arts. The teacher exposes participants in studio art classes to a range of artistic media, some as complex as etching or lithography, while using the collections of the museum to demonstrate these processes to the students. In the one-time visit programs and multi-session seminars, curriculum is usually well defined by the head of outreach education and must be followed by the Teacher. These programs usually combine studio ex-

ercises with art-historical lectures and open discussion as a means of helping children understand and articulate the meaning of a work of art, or an art-historical period. A single visit to the museum may include all of these elements, which are developed more thoroughly in multi-session seminars.

Outreach education programs depend for their success on cooperation between museum staff and the school system's teachers and administrators. In some outreach programs the museum's Teachers work directly in the schools as well as in their own institutions. It is important that the museum staff win the trust of school officials and work with them closely to develop and implement programs.

In addition the Teacher may:
- assist the head of outreach education in fund-raising for outreach programs
- organize and implement teacher workshops to let schools know about the museum's programs

Salaries

A full-time Teacher averages a salary between $13,000 and $20,000. In a small museum it is likely that the salary will be at the low end of this range. Teachers may be hired part-time for a salary ranging from $1,000 to $10,000.

Employment Prospects

Although training in teaching is necessary, this position can be an entry-level job in a museum. Prospects are fair if the candidate combines proper training with flexibility and an excellent knowledge of the areas of interest covered by the museum. It is often easier to start by getting part-time teaching.

Advancement Prospects

The prospects for advancement for museum Teachers are only fair since their activity is limited to the implementation rather than the design of programs. However, if the Teacher is able to work closely with the head of outreach education in evaluating current programs and proposing new ones, prospects are better for a promotion to that position.

Education

An undergraduate degree in education with a concentration in art history is necessary. A teaching certificate or graduate degree in teaching or art history is desirable.

Experience and Skills

Since teaching in a museum context may be more unconventional than within a school, it is necessary for the Teacher to combine excellent teaching skills with creativity and flexibility about his or her profession. In addition, the Teacher must be able to work closely with colleagues in the school system and be adept at navigating the bureaucratic systems of public schools. An excellent knowledge of art history is necessary, as is a love for working with children.

DOCENT COORDINATOR

CAREER PROFILE

Duties: Train and schedule volunteer lecturers, or docents

Salary Range: $13,000 to $20,000

Employment Prospects: Fair

Advancement Prospects: Fair

Prerequisites:
  Education—Undergraduate degree in art history or related field
  Experience—Background in teaching and good organizational skills
  Special Skills—Creativity, diplomacy, good public speaking skills

CAREER LADDER

```
┌─────────────────────────────────┐
│    Head of Outreach Education    │
│               or                 │
│    Head of Public Programming    │
└─────────────────────────────────┘

┌─────────────────────────────────┐
│                                  │
│        Docent Coordinator        │
│                                  │
└─────────────────────────────────┘

┌─────────────────────────────────┐
│                                  │
│    Docent, Teacher or Intern     │
│                                  │
└─────────────────────────────────┘
```

Position Description

In a large museum with an active outreach program or a high volume of visiting adult groups, special volunteers called docents are used as museum lecturers. The Docent Coordinator, who is directly supervised by the head of outreach education, is responsible for training docents and scheduling their activities. In some cases the Docent Coordinator is also a museum lecturer who, under supervision of the head of public programming, leads gallery talks and even gives courses or workshops for the public. Depending upon the size of the museum's docent program, this position may be part-time or it may be included in the responsibilities of the head of outreach education.

The docent gives introductory lectures in the museum's galleries covering aspects of its permanent collection or temporary exhibitions. These presentations vary in structure depending on the audience—whether of schoolchildren or an adult group. In most museums docents are given specialized training if they are interested in working with children. The Docent Coordinator is responsible for designing and implementing initial docent training, and providing a series of updates as they are required for temporary exhibitions or other changes in the museum's program. The Docent Coordinator also schedules group visits and provides docents for them. In some cases docents may offer informal tours weekly or daily in the galleries which are open to museum visitors.

Once or twice a year the Docent Coordinator offers a multi-session training seminar for new docents. This course provides art-historical background appropriate to the museum's areas of interest as well as insights into either public speaking strategies appropriate for adult groups or developmental educational theories for children. In most museums, docents are trained to lecture about specific aspects of the permanent collection so that they will gain experience in a particualr area and refine their skills. After this initial training session, the Docent Coordinator regularly updates his or her volunteers through meetings where art-historical materials and lectures are offered. Often, special educational events, like visits to other museums, are organized for docent groups. Whenever a temporary exhibition opens, the Docent Coordinator provides a special series of seminars to prepare docents to lead tours through it.

An effective, enthusiastic team of docents is an important educational resource for the museum. The Docent Coordinator must recruit and cultivate dedicated volunteers who will help interpret the museum's collections and programs.

In addition the Docent Coordinator may:

• administer other outreach education programs

• provide secretarial or clerical support for the head of outreach education

• offer special courses or seminars for the general public

Salaries

A full-time Docent Coordinator averages a salary between $13,000 and $20,000. In a small museum it is likely that the salary will be at the low end of this range. Docent Coordinators may be hired part-time for a fee or salary ranging from $2,000 to $10,000.

Employment Prospects

The Docent Coordinator may be an entry-level position, sometimes offered to an exceptional docent or intern. However, since a good knowledge of art history, plus research skills and teaching strategies, is necessary, the candidate must have appropriate informal and formal training. It may also be possible to begin working part-time as a Docent Coordinator, leading to other jobs within the education department.

Advancement Prospects

Advancement prospects for the Docent Coordinator are only fair, since his or her activity is confined within a relatively narrow scope. Nevertheless, the position provides a good introduction to both outreach education and public programming, and an excellent performance may lead to the position of head of public programming or head of outreach education.

Education

An undergraduate degree in art history is necessary, and coursework in teaching or museum education is invaluable. A graduate degree in art history or educaton is also a boon.

Experience and Skills

The Docent Coordinator must combine an excellent knowledge of art history with research and organizational skills. Although the curriculum for docent training is developed in conjunction with the head of outreach education, the Docent Coordinator is in charge of the extensive administrative duties involved with scheduling meetings and matching visiting groups with docents. In addition, it is extremely important that the Docent Coordinator enjoy working with people and be able to communicate his or her enthusiasm effectively. When working with volunteers it is necessary to convey a sense of appreciation for their work and of their value to the institution. As much as art-historical knowledge and administrative efficiency, an ability to nourish the volunteer is essential to this job.

CURATOR FOR EDUCATION

CAREER PROFILE

Duties: Supervise the design and implementation of all education programs

Alternate Titles: Director of Education, Educator

Salary Range: $20,000 to $60,000 +

Employment Prospects: Poor to fair

Advancement Prospects: Good

Prerequisites:

Education—Undergraduate and advanced degrees in art history, education or museum studies

Background—Extensive experience in museum outreach and public programming; administrative experience

Special Skills—Ability to assess educational needs and design appropriate programs; excellent knowledge of art history

CAREER LADDER

```
┌─────────────────────────────────────┐
│                                      │
│              Director                │
│                                      │
└─────────────────────────────────────┘

┌─────────────────────────────────────┐
│                                      │
│       Curator for Education          │
│                                      │
└─────────────────────────────────────┘

┌─────────────────────────────────────┐
│    Head of Public Programming        │
│                 or                   │
│    Head of Outreach Education        │
└─────────────────────────────────────┘
```

Position Description

The Curator for Education develops, implements, administers and evaluates the museum's education programs. As head of one of the museum's major departments, the Curator for Education supervises as many as 30 employees in a large museum. Museum education encompasses interpretive materials in the galleries, lectures, courses, classes and workshops, as well as outreach to schoolchildren and other special populations like the elderly or the handicapped. The Curator for Education sets a policy for the museum's educational activity and works with his or her staff to fund and implement programs.

Educational activity in a museum is closely related to the institution's collections and exhibition policies. The Curator for Education works closely with the director and curators to develop specific programs like didactic brochures and special orientation areas featuring slide shows and videotapes, as well as lectures and courses that will help museum visitors understand the history and meaning of the exhibited art objects. Once this policy is set, the head of public programming carries it out in concert with the Curator for Education.

As he or she assists the head of public programming in creating a policy for programming, the Curator for Education also works with the head of outreach educa-

tion. He or she takes responsibility for some of the administrative work of creating liaisons with school department officials and education specialists. As the administrative head of the education department, the Curator for Education must work closely with federal and state funding agencies to procure funding for outreach and public programs.

The Curator for Education is the primary spokesperson within the museum and in the community for the educational activities of the institution. He or she must develop a budget for the department, attract funding and evaluate performance of the various programs to the director and trustees of the institution. It is also important for the Curator for Education to stay abreast of new developments in museum education through participation in professional organizations, and to stay aware of the evolving exhibition policies of the museum in order to set proper educational policies to interpret them.

In addition the Curator for Education may:

- organize and implement education programs in addition to planning and administering them

- organize special didactic exhibitions

- edit an educational newsletter or publication for museum members or the general public

Salaries

Curators for Education make an average salary between $20,000 and $40,000. Salaries are closely related to the size of the department and the degree of administrative responsibility. The Curator for Education may make as much as $60,000.

Employment Prospects

The Curator for Education is one of the most sought-after jobs in a museum and competition is extremely strong. Applicants need a combination of an impressive educational background and extensive experience in museum education or curatorial work. Since this position is a desirable one, with a great deal of responsibility, turnover is minimal, making prospects even more difficult.

Advancement Prospects

The Curator for Education is the head of a department, so advancement within the education area is not possible. However, the Curator for Education may be able to advance to the position of director, depending upon the objectives and policies of the institution. It is also possible to advance to the position of Curator for Education at a larger museum.

Education

An advanced degree in education or in an area of the museum's specialization or in museum studies is typically necessary, as well as an undergraduate degree in art history or education. Teacher training and coursework in writing and public speaking are helpful.

Experience and Skills

The Curator for Education must have a good knowledge of art history as well as a knowledge of museum education techniques and resources. He or she must be aware of the objectives, curricula and operation of school systems and other educational institutions. Since there is a good deal of public interaction built into this job, the Curator for Education must have excellent speaking and writing skills as well as a strong enthusiasm for the objectives and programs of the museum. The Curator for Education must be adept at research and be aware of the formal means of evaluating educational programs. Since this is a position which requires the design of museum policy, the Curator for Education must have a wide knowledge of his or her field, as well as the ability and vision necessary to set a direction and organize a staff to implement it.

HEAD OF OUTREACH EDUCATION

CAREER PROFILE

Duties: Design and supervise museum outreach programs for children, the elderly, the handicapped or other under-served populations

Salary Range: $17,000 to $35,000

Employment Prospects: Poor to fair

Advancement Prospects: Good

Prerequisites:

Education—Undergraduate degree in art history and graduate degree in education or museum studies

Experience—Background in teaching art and designing curricula

Special Skills—Administrative ability, creativity, knowledge of current educational theories

CAREER LADDER

```
┌─────────────────────────────┐
│   Curator for Education      │
└─────────────────────────────┘

┌─────────────────────────────┐
│  Head of Outreach Education  │
└─────────────────────────────┘

┌─────────────────────────────┐
│         Teacher              │
└─────────────────────────────┘
```

Position Description

Outreach is one of the primary areas of educational activity in a museum. Through its outreach programs an institution actively recruits special populations, like schoolchildren, the elderly or the handicapped, by designing special educational programs for them. The Head of Outreach Education works with the curator for education to develop an outreach policy, and then he or she designs and implements individual programs.

In most museums the primary outreach audience is schoolchildren. Museums may provide many different types of program, from a single, highly-structured visit to the museum to multiple-session seminars which involve a small number of students in an extended art experience. Most inner-city art museums make special efforts to serve minority students within their area. In developing programs with local school systems, the Head of Outreach Education must be sensitive to the needs of collaborating schools and be able to tailor the museum's education programs to their goals. Often the success or failure of outreach education depends on the ability of the person in this position to gain the trust of the teachers and school system administrators, as well as the public funding necessary to implement programs. The Head of Outreach Education represents the museum in the educational world and must be adept at communicating its outreach goals and offerings.

In order to design effective programs, the Head of Outreach Education must be aware of developmental theories for the age groups of children served by the museum, as well as knowing the standard museum educational models. Using this knowledge, he or she is able to develop a specific curriculum for school-children, relating works in the museum's permanent collection or in temporary exhibitions to subjects they learn in school. The Head of Outreach Education either teaches these programs personally or trains and supervises a group of teachers who do. Museum education ranges from very conservative lecture-oriented programs to experimental methods of teaching which involve open discussion and creative exercises.

Although children are the museum's primary outreach audience, many institutions broaden their activity by using art either as a tool for students who need remedial help or as a therapeutic experience for the handicapped. Many museums even have programs for the blind. The Head of Outreach Education may also organize visits to the museum by community groups, nursing home residents or any other population interested in an interpretive experience within the museum.

In addition the Head of Outreach Education may:
- attend workshops or conferences on educational theory

- perform significant fund-raising for outreach education programs, especially to public funding agencies
- organize special workshops for teachers to communicate the programs of the museum

Salaries

Although salaries can be as low as $12,000, they average between $17,000 and $30,000 and can be as high as $45,000.

Employment Prospects

As in all museum education positions, competition is tough for Head of Outreach Education. It is unlikely for an applicant to be hired without extensive teaching experience and/or a graduate degree in education with a specialization in museum studies. Proven ability to build curricula is also necessary. Even with these qualifications, there are only a limited number of jobs available and many people interested in them.

Advancement Prospects

Prospects are good for a Head of Outreach Education to become the curator for education. Outreach is a fundamental community service performed by the museum which gives this position a good deal of visibility and prestige. The possibilities of getting a position in a larger museum with greater outreach activity are also good.

Education

The Head of Outreach Education should have an undergraduate degree in art history or a related field, and a graduate level degree in education or museum studies, as well as specific training in teaching.

Experience and Skills

The Head of Outreach Education must have an excellent knowledge of the educational principles and models appropriate to the populations served by the museum, as well as teaching experience and expertise. It is fundamental that he or she be adept at negotiating with school administrators and teachers as well as the public funding agencies which typically make outreach programs possible. Excellent verbal and written skills are a great benefit. In order to stay abreast of new educational developments, the Head of Outreach Education must have research skills and memberships in educational associations. As with any teaching-related position, this job requires an empathy for and enthusiasm about the populations served.

EDITOR

Duties: Coordinate the production and editing of museum publications

Alternate Titles: Head of Publications, Publication Coordinator

Salary Range: $8,000 to $30,000+

Employment Prospects: Poor to fair

Prerequisites:

Education—Undergraduate degree in English or journalism

Experience—Knowledge of editorial procedures and publication production

Special Skills—Excellent writing skills and technical knowledge of grammar

```
┌─────────────────────────────────┐
│                                 │
│            Editor               │
│                                 │
└─────────────────────────────────┘

┌─────────────────────────────────┐
│                                 │
│   Assistant Editor in Museums   │
│       or Other Publishing       │
│                                 │
└─────────────────────────────────┘

┌─────────────────────────────────┐
│                                 │
│            College              │
│                                 │
└─────────────────────────────────┘
```

Position Description

Museums produce a great deal of written material, and in a large institution there is usually an Editor whose responsibility it is to supervise the creation of printed matter. In some cases the Editor is only concerned with scholarly and educational publications, leaving promotional and membership-related publishing to those departments. In other cases the Editor handles everything written that is prepared by the museum.

The Editor reads, corrects, rewrites or revises the material under his or her supervision to ensure that it is presented clearly, in precise language and proper grammatical form. This requires a close working relationship with the director, curators, the public relations officer and other museum professionals who generate publications. After editorial suggestions are made, the Editor is also responsible for proofreading copy after it is typeset and choosing a printing house.

The Editor works closely with the museum designer or a free-lancer if there is no full-time designer to adapt the institution's overall graphic image to each specific project. The Editor might also be responsible for carrying out the search for photographic material to illustrate a publication, or may be asked to commission the museum photographer or free-lancer to make photographs for a publication. The Editor must manage copyright procedures for museum publications and also apply for Library of Congress catalogue listings. If a publication involves an outside author the Editor may act as liaison with him or her.

More and more frequently major museums are publishing their catalogues in conjunction with a university or art press. The Editor must attempt to create this sort of partnership and carry through on it. He or she may also be involved with distributing museum publications, especially catalogues of the important exhibitions, by publishing a promotional newsletter with listings of available books.

In addition the Editor may:

- prepare public relations releases about upcoming publications
- write a great deal of copy for the museum, from promotional texts to essays in art history
- advise the Curator for Education on lecture programs
- edit a journal published by the museum

Salary

Editors make on the average between $15,000 and $30,000. They may make as much as $47,000 or as little as $8,000.

Employment Prospects

Both editorial and museum work are highly desirable individually, so their combination can be even more competitive. A prospective Editor needs to have not only an expert grasp of grammar, but also a considerable knowledge of art history. Not every museum has a separate publications department, which makes available opportunities even fewer.

Advancement Prospects

Unless the Editor has curatorial ambitions, there are not many places he or she can move within the museum. Managing a large publications department, however, can prepare the Editor for a better job in publishing, either in a university setting or with a company that specializes in art publications. The Editor might also obtain a job as a magazine or journal editor on an art publication.

Education

The Editor should have a degree in either English or journalism, with significant coursework in the area of the museum's specialization, or a degree in art history, with demonstrated technical language skills.

Experience and Skills

Although editorial work requires an expert knowledge of grammar, an excellent grasp of stylistic form, and the ability to use language precisely, a good Editor must have more than this technical knowledge. He or she must have the ability to understand the intention of the author and, when necessary, rephrase his or her words so they read more precisely. This usually requires an excellent knowledge of the field under consideration as well as superior writing skills. The Editor must be able to proofread accurately and be throughly aware of copyright law, as well as being familiar with the publishing industry, preferably with experience at an outside press. Experience in distributing special-interest books is valuable.

HEAD OF PUBLIC PROGRAMMING

CAREER PROFILE

Duties: Organize and administer museum lectures, symposia, workshops and gallery talks

Salary Range: $17,000 to $35,000

Employment Prospects: Poor to fair

Advancement Prospects: Good

Prerequsites:

Education—Undergraduate degree in art history; graduate degree is a benefit

Experience—Background in research and administration; very good academic knowledge of the field

Special Skills—Good ability to get along with people, excellent organizational skills and speaking style

CAREER LADDER

```
┌─────────────────────────────────────┐
│                                      │
│        Curator for Education         │
│                                      │
└─────────────────────────────────────┘

┌─────────────────────────────────────┐
│                                      │
│      Head of Public Programming      │
│                                      │
└─────────────────────────────────────┘

┌─────────────────────────────────────┐
│                                      │
│        Lecturer or College or        │
│          Graduate Training           │
│                                      │
└─────────────────────────────────────┘
```

Position Description

The Head of Public Programming plans, organizes and implements the museum's lectures, symposia, workshops, gallery talks and other academic events. In most museums lectures interpret and enrich the institution's permanent collection, or temporary exhibitions, so the Head of Public Programming must monitor curatorial planning and stay abreast of the issues relevant to the museum's areas of interest, and the academic experts working in those areas. In smaller museums, a curator may have responsibility for public programs.

Most museums program several types of lecture events, meant to appeal to a variety of audiences. Typically, gallery talks by curators, artists or art historians are frequently available for museum visitors. Special lectures by experts are organized for audiences intersted in issues of art history and criticism; and academic symposia may be presented for a highly trained audience of art historians and curators. Courses and workshops in areas relevant to the museum's collections are offered to laymen interested in learning more about art. The Head of Public Programming must be adept at identifying these different audiences and tailoring programs to their interests. He or she must also be able to find appropriate speakers for each context.

After designing a policy for public programming in cooperation with the curator for education and the curatorial staff, the Head of Public Programming is responsible for implementing his or her events. After initial research to identify potential speakers, the Head of Public Programming contacts them by phone or letter to negotiate fees and conditions of the lecture or event. He or she is responsible for preparing promotional materials and working with the public relations officer to disperse them. It is also his or her responsibility to coordinate audiovisual equipment on the evening of the event and to entertain visiting lecturers.

The Head of Public Programming is one of the most academic positions within a museum. He or she must read widely within the fields of interest of the institution, and maintain a network of contacts among art historians, artists and critics.

In addition the Head of Public Programming may:

- document lecture events through written transcripts or videotapes
- teach or lecture in gallery talks and courses
- supervise museum docents if there is not a docent coordinator
- design interpretive materials for museum galleries, like brochures, slide shows or videotapes

Salaries

Although salaries can be as low as $12,000, they average between $17,000 and $30,000, and can be as high as $45,000.

Employment Prospects

The Head of Public Programming is one of the most desirable positions in the museum; it combines a significant involvement in art history and contact with experts in the field. Competition is very stiff. Applicants must have extensive knowledge of the museum's areas of interest as well as academic or critical contacts. Excellent writing skills and an impressive body of personal publications are helpful.

Advancement Prospects

The Head of Public Programming has good prospects for becoming the curator for education. It is also possible, depending upon his or her interests and the structure of the museum, for the Head of Public Programming to enter the curatorial area. Lecture programs can be an innovative aspect of the museum's activities, so it is possible to distinguish oneself in this field.

Education

An undergraduate degree in art history or a related field is necessary, and an advanced degree in a similar area of museum studies is an advantage—in some museums, a requirement. Having written a thesis or published articles while in school would be helpful.

Experience and Skills

The Head of Public Programming must be adept at all kinds of research, both academic and informal. He or she must be able to grasp concepts perceptively and quickly. Since the Head of Public Programming works closely with experts in many fields related to the museum's work, strong communications skills are necessary. This position also requires excellent writing skills and the ability to work efficiently and quickly. Since the Head of Public Programming handles the administrative details of organizing lectures, paying lecturers, assisting with publicizing their talks and providing special audiovisual aids, he or she must be an effective administrator.

BOOKSTORE MANAGER

CAREER PROFILE

Duties: Supervise finances and personnel of museum bookstore; buy books and gifts

Salary Range: $10,000 to $40,000

Employment Prospects: Fair to good

Advancement Prospects: Fair

Prerequisites:

Education—Undergraduate degree in business or retailing

Experience—Knowledge of accounting and the publishing industry

Special Skills—Salesmanship, knowledge of art history and art books

CAREER LADDER

```
┌─────────────────────────┐
│   Director of Finance   │
└─────────────────────────┘

┌─────────────────────────┐
│    Bookstore Manager    │
└─────────────────────────┘

┌─────────────────────────┐
│      Salesperson        │
└─────────────────────────┘
```

Position Description

Most museums, whether large or small, have a bookstore. These shops contribute to the institution's earned income and provide the community with periodicals, catalogues and books on the arts that may be difficult to obtain elsewhere. The Bookstore Manager either personally buys the books and gifts sold in the shop or supervises buyers who do; and he or she manages the budget, accounting procedures and personnel for the store. In large museums a store may gross millions of dollars per year, and the Bookstore Manager must be an experienced retailer, whereas in smaller museums the job might be filled by someone interested in art books and with a talent for administrative detail.

Since museum bookstores stock special interest books the Bookstore Manager must constantly research new publications that might be appropriate to the store. Especially in a smaller operation, works in stock usually relate to the collections or activities of the museum. This means browsing in art bookstores in different cities, searching through publishers' lists and attending book conventions. Most museum stores also carry inexpensive gift items, stationery and postcards, so the Manager must attend gift shows and meet with sales representatives to develop stock.

Major exhibitions are frequently accompanied by special sales desks placed directly outside the galleries. These temporary sales areas include museum publications, like catalogues related to the exhibition, as well as supplementary books, souvenirs and postcards. The Bookstore Manager must supervise the creation of these special stores and evaluate their profitability.

Usually the Bookstore Manager reports to the director of finance and must be well aware of retail accounting and inventory procedures. He or she works with the director of finance to create a budget for the shop, including expenses and projected sales. Inventory may be taken quarterly, semiannually or annually to keep track of stock, and invoices from vendors must be attended to daily.

In addition the Bookstore Manager may:
- prepare and advertise special sales in the store
- market museum publications to other bookstores
- manage direct mail marketing of museum products, including preparation of a catalogue
- assist in publication of posters and postcards of objects in the museum's collection or in temporary exhibitions

Salary

Salaries vary widely depending on the scale of the shop. As an entry-level position in a small museum, the salary might be as low as $10,000 to $15,000, whereas the Manager of a major museum store could make $40,000.

Employment Prospects

Employment prospects vary widely depending on the size of the museum store. Retailing experience and extensive knowledge of art books is necessary for a large shop, whereas the position of Bookstore Manager may be an entry-level one at a small museum. Competition is reasonably difficult for a small museum and tougher in a larger one.

Advancement Prospects

Since the Bookstore Manager is involved in the earned-income effort of a museum and has significant experience in accounting procedures, it is possible for him or her to advance to a position in the financial department and eventually to director of finance. This is not terribly likely, however, especially in a small museum. Prospects are good that the Bookstore Manager could get a better retail position outside of the museum.

Education

An undergraduate degree in business or retailing, or in art history with coursework in business, is necessary. If the museum store is particularly large, an advanced degree in business is desirable.

Experience and Skills

The Bookstore Manager must have a good knowledge of art books and, preferably, art history. He or she must know where to research the availability of publications, gift items, stationery and postcards. This position requires an excellent grasp of retail principles, including a knowledge of display, accounting and inventory procedures. As in all retail jobs, the Bookstore Manager must have a highly developed sense of the market he or she is reaching, and a creative and flexible attitude toward acquiring stock which will appeal to this market. Experience in direct mail marketing is valuable, especially in large museums.

EXHIBIT DESIGNER

CAREER PROFILE

Duties: Design installations of permanent museum galleries and temporary exhibitions

Salary Range: $18,000 to $30,000 +

Employment Prospects: Fair to good

Advancement Prospects: Fair to good

Prerequsites:

Education—Degree in graphic or industrial design, or environmental architecture

Experience—Background in exhibit design

Special Skills—Sensitivity to art; excellent knowledge of graphic design styles and techniques

CAREER LADDER

```
┌─────────────────────────────────┐
│        Chief Curator or         │
│       Director of Finance       │
└─────────────────────────────────┘

┌─────────────────────────────────┐
│                                 │
│        Exhibit Designer         │
│                                 │
└─────────────────────────────────┘

┌─────────────────────────────────┐
│                                 │
│  College or Assistant Designer  │
│                                 │
└─────────────────────────────────┘
```

Position Description

Museums interpret works of art in many different ways. One of the most direct is through gallery installations which either establish connections between related artworks or create a chronological or historical context through written wall labels or other types of documentation. Although in small and even medium-size museums curators typically design exhibitions, most large museums employ an Exhibit Designer whose job it is to translate curatorial and educational ideas into gallery installations.

Especially when a museum is planning a large temporary exhibition, or an installation of objects from the permanent collection, the Exhibit Designer must work closely with curators to translate their concept to the galleries. After consultations, the Exhibit Designer creates preliminary plans, renderings and scale models, showing the configuration of walls to be built in the gallery space, placement of works, and any special pedestals, cabinets or cases which need to be fabricated for the exhibition. The Exhibit Designer decides on the color to be used on gallery walls and works with the graphic designer to create signs for the exhibition.

Not only must the Exhibit Designer have a highly refined understanding of art objects and how they interact with one another in terms of color and scale, but he or she must also be aware of the principles of conservation and preservation of artworks so that they may

be installed with proper light and safety precautions. The Exhibit Designer works closely with the preparator and his or her crew to fabricate special exhibition cabinets, cases, pedestals or display tables; a knowledge of and experience with the techniques of exhibit production is thus necessary.

The Exhibit Designer supervises the installation of the exhibition or permanent installation and designs proper lighting once artworks are in place. Lighting art objects correctly is a special skill in which the Exhibit Designer must be expert. He or she may also be involved with designing special educational presentations, like an orientation room or didactic gallery space.

In addition the Exhibit Designer may:
• act as graphic designer for the museum
• personally fabricate special exhibition materials like cabinets and display cases
• manage the budget for gallery installations

Salaries

An Exhibit Designer makes an average salary between $18,000 and $30,000, but may make as much as $50,000 in a large museum.

Employment Prospects

Only medium- and large-sized museums employ full-time Exhibit Designers, so positions are limited and usually require considerable experience. With an appropriate degree and a portfolio of relevant design work prospects are fair.

Advancement Prospects

Since the Exhibit Designer must synthesize many skills—a sensitivity to art history, a practical knowledge of design, and an awareness of fabrication techniques—a good one has excellent chances to advance to a better job in a different museum or to launch a free-lance career.

Education

A degree or certificate in graphic design, industrial design, commercial arts, or architecture and interior design is necessary. Coursework in studio arts, typography and theater design are beneficial.

Experience and Skills

The Exhibit Designer must be able to take a concept from the curator of an exhibition or permanent installation and translate it into a coherent, appealing presentation. This requires an excellent grasp of art concepts and the ability to make refined aesthetic judgments, as well as excellent communications skills and the ability to compromise. The Exhibit Designer must know how to make renderings and scale models as well as how to fabricate actual exhibition furnishings like cabinets and pedestals. He or she needs a working knowledge of conservation principles and a familiarity with lighting design. Since the Exhibit Designer often supervises the preparator and his or her crew and manages the budget for an installation, he or she must have good administrative skills.

GRAPHIC DESIGNER

CAREER PROFILE

Duties: Design printed materials and museum signs

Salary Range: $18,000 to $30,000 +

Employment Prospects: Fair

Advancement Prospects: Fair

Prerequisites:
   Education—Undergraduate degree in graphic arts
   Experience—Background in designing a range of publications
   Special Skills—Knowledge of art history; creativity

CAREER LADDER

```
┌─────────────────────────────┐
│                             │
│     Director of Finance     │
│                             │
└─────────────────────────────┘

┌─────────────────────────────┐
│                             │
│      Graphic Designer       │
│                             │
└─────────────────────────────┘

┌─────────────────────────────┐
│                             │
│  College or Assistant Designer  │
│                             │
└─────────────────────────────┘
```

Position Description

Museums publish in several formats. Invitations to openings and special events, newsletters/calendars, didactic brochures and exhibition catalogues are all important marketing and educational tools. In a large- or medium-size museum with a good deal of publishing activity, an in-house Designer helps to manage design and printing and works to create a unified graphic image for the museum.

In most museums several different departments prepare written materials for museum members, visitors and the general public. It is important that the Graphic Designer balance the objectives of each publication with the need to establish a coherent graphic image for the institution. This is a primary public relations and marketing strategy which enhances the museum's visibility in the community. The Graphic Designer may work with the director and other high-level management of the museum to develop general design principles which are followed in all of the museum's printed materials.

To develop an appropriate design, the Graphic Designer works on each printed piece with the person in charge of the project. This usually involves a preliminary presentation of ideas followed by more developed mock-ups of the piece submitted for final approval. In a complex project like a newsletter or exhibition catalogue the preliminary development of a design may take several weeks. The Graphic Designer then negotiates with printers and supervises the reproduction and printing of the piece. He or she must create a schedule for the production of all museum publications and be sure that deadlines are met. The Graphic Designer usually supervises the museum photographer, who contributes photographs to the publications.

With curators and the exhibition designer, the Graphic Designer conceives all printed materials accompanying an exhibition, like didactic wall labels, object labels and special graphics for title walls. More and more frequently, large museums advertise their major exhibitions with banners on the front of the building or at other sites throughout the city. The Graphic Designer is responsible for creating these materials.

In addition, the Graphic Designer may:

* design print advertisements for the museum
* assist in designing exhibitions if there is no exhibit designer
* work with outside advertising agencies on special promotional campaigns for the museum
* design museum stationery and other office materials

Salaries

A museum Graphic Designer will average a salary between $18,000 and $30,000 and may make as much as $50,000 in a large museum with a busy publications program. Even museums without a full-time Graphic

Designer need design services. Free-lance fees can range from $25 to $100 per hour.

Employment Prospects

Since the business of museums is art, it takes a special designer to create an appropriate graphic image for this kind of institution. Experience with a wide variety of publications is a great benefit, as is a sensitivity to art. Since many designers find museum work attractive, competition is tough.

Advancement Prospects

If there is only one Graphic Designer in a museum, there is little chance of advancement. However, doing design work for an arts organization is a good way to gain free-lance jobs elsewhere, or advance to a job with more responsibility in another museum.

Education

An undergraduate or graduate degree in graphic design is absolutely necessary. A liberal arts degree or coursework in art history is invaluable.

Experience and Skills

Excellent design skills and a knowledge of every aspect of the production process of printed materials, from mock-up through typesetting and printing, is essential. Supplementary art classes or art history will stand the Designer in good stead. Since this job includes a good deal of organizational responsibility and interaction with museum staff as well as outside vendors, the Graphic Designer must have excellent communications skills. As in all areas of graphic design the ability to understand a client's intention and articulate his or her visual ideas is of the utmost importance.

LIBRARIAN

CAREER PROFILE

Duties: Manage the museum's library of books and slides

Salary Range: $15,000 to $30,000+

Employment Prospects: Fair

Advancement Prospects: Fair

Prerequisites:
    Education—Advanced degree in library science, undergraduate degree in art history or related field
    Experience—Background in library work, knowledge of art history
    Special Skills—Excellent research skills, knowledge of foreign languages

CAREER LADDER

```
┌─────────────────────────────────┐
│   Director or Chief Curator      │
│    or Director of Finance        │
└─────────────────────────────────┘

┌─────────────────────────────────┐
│          Librarian               │
└─────────────────────────────────┘

┌─────────────────────────────────┐
│  College or Assistant Librarian  │
└─────────────────────────────────┘
```

Position Description

Many large museums maintain their own library as an in-house resource for the curators and the education staff as well as for visiting museum professionals, scholars and members of the general public. The Librarian administers the museum library, manages the acquisition and cataloguing of books, periodicals and manuscripts, and performs a variety of services related to written or visual materials for the museum staff.

The Librarian must keep abreast of the materials published in the museum's areas of concentration. Often the library includes not only books and magazines but also visual resources like slides, black-and-white photographs and videotapes, which may be used by members of the education staff to illustrate lectures, or by curators as aids in organizing exhibitions. Often the Librarian is asked by members of curatorial departments to conduct background research for a particular exhibition or special project. In some cases the Librarian is also the curator of a museum's graphics or illustrated book collection.

A museum's archives are usually catalogued and preserved in its library. Materials like exhibition files, correspondence, transcripts of lectures and museum publications form an important resource for art historians as well as the museum staff. The Librarian controls access to this information and also develops copyright and reproduction policy for archival material. He or she may be called upon to answer the inquiries of scholars or art critics into the museum's history.

The Librarian may also work closely with the registrar to catalogue the institution's collections. He or she can assist staff members who edit museum publications by verifying facts or helping with copy editing and proofreading.

In addition the Librarian may:

- publish articles interpreting the museum's archives or publish actual documents

- advise the public relations staff about museum history on the occasion of special anniversaries or celebrations

- assist curators in organizing special exhibitions or in preparing didactic materials for them

Salaries

On the average, museum Librarians make between $15,000 and $30,000, but salaries can be as high as $60,000.

Employment Prospects

Generally it is only large museums that maintain their own libraries, so opportunities are limited. Moreover, it is necessary that the Librarian have considerable knowledge of art history as well as training in library sciences. Even with appropriate education competition is tough.

Advancement Prospects

As in many areas of museum work, once one has broken into an area, prospects are good that advancement will occur. There may be only one Librarian in a museum, so movement up the ladder may mean a job in a large museum or another art library. It is also possible that the Librarian may move into a curatorial or registrarial position, depending upon his or her ambitions and skills.

Education

An advanced degree in library science is necessary and an undergraduate degree in art history is highly desirable. Coursework in computer systems and in writing or English is helpful.

Experience and Skills

The Librarian must have excellent research skills, including the ability to provide bibliographic support and familiarity with computerized information services. Knowledge of a foreign language is a great asset. He or she must be completely versed in the aspects of librarianship: acquisitions, cataloguing, reference and administration. A broad knowledge of art history is invaluable, as is the ability to handle detail skillfully.

Organizations and Associations

The professional association for librarians is the American Library Association (see Appendix IV).

PHOTOGRAPHER

CAREER PROFILE

Duties: Photograph art objects and museum installations

Salary Range: $15,000 to $25,000

Employment Prospects: Poor to fair

Prerequisites:
  Education—Technical training in studio photography

  Experience—Background in photographing works of art

  Special Skills—Sensitivity to art objects; knowledge of lighting; versatility

CAREER LADDER

```
┌─────────────────────────────┐
│        Registrar or         │
│     Director of Finance     │
└─────────────────────────────┘

┌─────────────────────────────┐
│        Photographer         │
└─────────────────────────────┘

┌─────────────────────────────┐
│         College or          │
│    Assistant Photographer   │
└─────────────────────────────┘
```

Position Description

Most large museums maintain a staff Photographer who produces documentary photographs of the museum's collection and installation photographs of its exhibitions. It is extraordinarily difficult to photograph art in such a way that the color, scale and presence of an object is conveyed in a single picture, so the Photographer must be sensitive to the original works and expert in lighting and other technical aspects of photography.

Every work of art a museum owns must be photographed for the registrar's records; in some cases, several pictures of a single object are required to communicate its essence. If an object is damaged, the Photographer must photograph the damaged area of the work for insurance purposes. Museum Photographers usually document temporary exhibitions by taking slides of gallery installations. In a contemporary museum he or she may also provide pictures of empty galleries for artists who will make a site-specific installation.

In addition to these ongoing tasks, the Photographer is regularly called upon to work on special projects. In some instances, he or she may research or re-photograph old pictures to be used as explanatory material in an exhibition. The Photographer plays an important role in museum publications by preparing illustrations for exhibition catalogues, newsletters and promotional literature. The Photographer may also be called upon to produce educational slide shows for the public or document events at the museum, like members' openings, benefit parties or special lectures.

The Photographer works closely with the museum's designer and public relations officer to maintain a visual record of what has happened at the museum. Usually he or she is responsible for maintaining the photographic files of programs and events sponsored by the institution. The Photographer must also run the museum's darkroom, including maintenance and purchase of equipment and materials.

In addition the Photographer may:

- assist in designing museum publications
- assist curators in obtaining photographs and conducting photographic research
- assist in developing newspaper or magazine advertisements for the museum

Salaries

Many museum Photographers, especially those who work for small institutions, are employed on a free-lance basis, making from $100 to $300 per day. Although this sounds lucrative, the museum may only need a photographer's services a few days every month. Staff photographers employed full-time make between $15,000 and $25,000 depending upon the extent of their responsibilities.

Employment Prospects

Generally it is only large museums with significant collections or a very active publications program that employ a full-time Photographer. Since the pay scale for a museum Photographer is relatively low, it is

60 Career Opportunities in Art

possible to get a museum job on moderate experience. Some past work with art objects is essential.

Advancement Prospects

Unless the Photographer has a good deal of art-historical knowledge, or another type of skill attractive to the museum, it is unlikely that he or she will be able to advance within the organization. However, once a Photographer has worked for an institution it is easier to get free-lance work from artists, galleries or other museums. For someone interested in the arts, a job as a museum photographer is a good first step toward a free-lance career. If the Photographer has design skills he or she may advance to the position of museum designer.

Education

Although a college degree in photography or liberal arts is attractive, a high school diploma and certified technical training in photography, with an emphasis on studio photography and the use of large-format equipment, is sufficient. Apprenticeship training may be acceptable or desirable.

Experience and Skills

Some experience in commercial photography and processing as well as studio experience is necessary. Since the Photographer often works on several projects at once, good organizational and administrative skills will come in handy. A familiarity with art history and experience with handling art objects are invaluable to a museum Photographer. Since he or she often works under tight deadlines, it is important for the Photographer to be efficient, tactful and coolheaded. It is also necessary that the person in this job be able to manage a darkroom.

PREPARATOR

Duties: Install temporary and permanent installations

Alternate Title: Installation Manager

Salary Range: $15,000 to $30,000 +

Employment Prospects: Fair

Advancement Prospects: Fair

Prerequisites:

Education—Undergraduate degree preferred; training in carpentry

Experience—Background in handling and installing art; excellent carpentry skills

Special Skills—Problem-solving ability, good interpersonal skills

```
┌─────────────────────────────────┐
│   Registrar or Chief Curator or │
│      Director of Finance        │
└─────────────────────────────────┘

┌─────────────────────────────────┐
│          Preparator             │
└─────────────────────────────────┘

┌─────────────────────────────────┐
│      Exhibition Technician      │
└─────────────────────────────────┘
```

Position Description

The Preparator is responsible for physically installing works of art in permanent installations or temporary exhibitions as well as constructing any cabinetry, pedestals or temporary walls necessary. He or she works closely with the exhibition designer, conservator and registrar to ensure the safe arrival of works of art in the galleries and their proper installation. When objects in the museum's collection travel (for a temporary exhibition elsewhere) the Preparator is usually responsible for building crates to protect them during transport.

In preparation for an installation in the galleries, the Preparator receives instructions or detailed plans from the museum's exhibition designer or, in a smaller museum, the curator responsible. He or she orders paint, lumber, hardware and other materials necessary for the installation and begins any construction that can be done in advance. Once works of art begin to arrive the Preparator transports them to the galleries or to museum storage until installation occurs. He or she is also responsible for preparing objects for exhibition. For instance, if a portfolio of photographs arrives, the Preparator will prepare mats for them and then frame them, or exhibit them under a piece of Plexiglas or glass.

No matter how well planned an installation is, it is always a hectic time when instructions from the designer and curator must be realized under a strict deadline. The Preparator works with a crew which he or she hires, usually part-time, and must be adept at assigning tasks to them so that the many details associated with a museum installation are carried out efficiently. In addition to hanging paintings, installing sculptures or framing photographs, the Preparator is often responsible for fabricating didactic materials like object labels or documentary photographs.

The Preparator must work in concert with the registrar to log in incoming and outgoing objects and assess their condition. When an institution has no conservator, the Preparator will usually have some knowledge of conservation techniques. Even when there is someone in this position, the Preparator can assist in restoring or treating art objects. The Preparator supervises, stocks and maintains the budget for the museum workshop, and should have excellent carpentry skills.

In addition the Preparator may:

* assist the registrar in arranging transportation for art objects
* assist in building maintenance, especially carpentry
* participate in the planning stages of an installation in order to help curators design installations

• work directly with a living artist to prepare an exhibition of his or her work

Salaries

The Preparator makes between $15,000 and $30,000 and can make a higher salary in a major museum.

Employment Prospects

Employment prospects are fair. It is necessary that a Preparator have experience in handling art objects and excellent carpentry skills. One way of improving one's chances for this position is to work on the installation crew in order to learn the necessary skills. In larger museums the Preparator and his crew are union workers so jobs are a bit harder to get.

Advancement Prospects

Unless the Preparator has excellent skills in the areas of conservation and registration, it is unlikely that he or she will rise in the museum. If these skills are possessed by the Preparator, it is possible to advance to conservator or registrar.

Education

Training in carpentry is necessary. Coursework in art history, art conservation, museum management or graphic design is helpful.

Experience and Skills

In addition to excellent knowledge of carpentry, the Preparator should have versatile problem-solving skills. He or she must be well acquainted with the hardware associated with installing works of art as well as the various techniques available. A professional knowledge of painting and framing is desirable. The Preparator must manage a crew effectively, so the ability to work efficiently and divide responsibility is imperative, as is the capacity to work well with other museum professionals. Some knowledge of budget management is desirable.

MEMBERSHIP OFFICER

Duties: Recruit and record museum members, plan special events for them

Alternate Titles: Director of Membership, Membership Secretary

Salary Range: $10,000 to $17,000+

Employment Prospects: Fair to good

Advancement Prospects: Fair

Prerequisites:
   Education—Undergraduate degree in business, marketing or related field

   Experience—Background in marketing, managing special events

   Special Skills—Good organizational skills, excellent interpersonal abilities

```
┌─────────────────────────────────────┐
│                                       │
│        Director of Development        │
│                                       │
└─────────────────────────────────────┘

┌─────────────────────────────────────┐
│                                       │
│         Membership Officer            │
│                                       │
└─────────────────────────────────────┘

┌─────────────────────────────────────┐
│                                       │
│    Department Assistant or College    │
│                                       │
└─────────────────────────────────────┘
```

Position Description

A museum's membership is one of its basic sources of support. For a yearly fee, members receive information about exhibitions and programs, discounts on special activities and free admission to the galleries. The Membership Officer is responsible for recruiting members and managing the planning and promotion of special members' events and educational programs, such as classes, films, workshops, lectures and openings.

Usually the Membership Officer reports to the director of development and is considered part of the fund-raising staff. However, in most museums, he or she works closely with the curator for education to provide educational as well as social experiences for museum members. In order to recruit new supporters, most museums print an informational brochure edited and written by the Membership Officer which describes the institution's areas of activity and special programs. This form of promotion is supplemented by direct-mail campaigns aimed at groups likely to join the museum. The Membership Officer must stay abreast of current marketing techniques and design effective ongoing promotions. He or she may also develop and deliver slide presentations about the museum to interested community groups.

The Membership Officer also coordinates special auxiliary or volunteer committees of the museum. He or she works with these groups to plan special events like lectures or benefit parties which contribute to the fund-raising effort of the institution. In many museums the Membership Officer is a position which requires a good deal of socializing with high-level museum supporters.

The administrative tasks involved with maintaining lists of members and potential members, direct-mail campaigns, mailings of newsletters and other information to members, as well as sending renewal letters when memberships lapse, are among the responsibilities of the Membership Officer. More and more frequently, museums are using sophisticated computer systems to maintain contact with their membership.

In addition the Membership Officer may:
- design and maintain a members' lounge in the museum
- assist the public relations officer in editing the museum's newsletter
- advise on marketing campaigns which may take place in other areas of the museum

Salaries

In some museums the Membership Officer is a low-level administrative position whose responsibilities are primarily clerical. Salaries in that case are as low as $10,000 and may rise to $15,000 or $17,000. When the Membership Officer has more substantive development responsibilities, salaries can be as high as $40,000.

Employment Prospects

Especially in a small museum, the Membership Officer can be an entry-level position with few requirements for special skills. Since the job is often one with high turnover, positions open up for people who are interested in the arts and who have a good head for detail. As museums focus more on earned income potential, Membership Officers will need more formal training in marketing and competition will increase.

Advancement Prospects

The Membership Officer has a fair chance of advancement within the museum. If he or she runs a successful recruitment campaign, attracts high-level donors to the museum and maintains a healthy membership in general, then the Membership Officer has a chance to advance to director of development. However, if responsibilities are primarily clerical, the potential for advancement is minimal.

Education

An undergraduate degree in business, public relations, marketing, public administration or liberal arts is appropriate for this position. Coursework in art history is preferred, and secretarial skills and proficiency on a computer are necessary.

Experience and Skills

It is important that the Membership Officer have a broad familiarity with nonprofit fund-raising. Knowledge of marketing techniques and the potential for using computers in a museum context is helpful. Since the Membership Officer is a liaison with the public, he or she should be comfortable both talking on the phone and explaining the programs and policies of the museum to groups. Writing skills and a knowledge of art history are critical.

GRANTS OFFICER

CAREER PROFILE

Duties: Process grant applications to government agencies, foundations and corporations

Alternate Titles: Development Associate, Assistant Director of Development

Salary Range: $15,000 to $22,000

Employment Prospects: Fair

Advancement Prospects: Good

Prerequisites:

Education—Undergraduate degree in arts administration or liberal arts

Experience—Background in grant writing and fund-raising

Special Skills—Excellent writing and organizational ability

CAREER LADDER

```
┌─────────────────────────────┐
│  Director of Development     │
└─────────────────────────────┘

┌─────────────────────────────┐
│  Grants Officer              │
└─────────────────────────────┘

┌─────────────────────────────┐
│  Department Assistant or     │
│  College                     │
└─────────────────────────────┘
```

Position Description

The Grants Officer is responsible for processing grant applications to government agencies, foundations and corporations. He or she also assists with or writes applications and maintains a reference library of potential funding sources, their guidelines and deadlines. Since most granting agencies require absolute compliance with their guidelines, the Grants Officer must be highly organized and attentive to detail. Responsibilities include typing, filing and other clerical duties related to grant applications.

In addition to program descriptions, government grants require a project budget, general financial information on the museum, and materials to illustrate the artistic content of the proposal, like slides, reviews, videotapes or records. The Grants Officer is responsible for gleaning the appropriate information from both the financial and curatorial staff. He or she must be able to coordinate a complex variety of information from several sources while under pressure to maintain deadlines. This requires tact, patience and organizational skills.

With the guidance of the director of development, to whom the Grants Officer reports, he or she must analyze potential funding sources to determine which of the museum's programs, if any, might be funded by them. This means obtaining and reading government funding agency guidelines, foundation annual reports and fund-raising newsletters to learn more about potential donors, and then following up on this information through telephone interviews with potential funders. Although grant project descriptions are typically written by the curatorial or other staff member who has conceived the project, the Grants Officer edits these proposals and tailors them to the priorities of a particular granting agency. Often several different proposals to different funders may be submitted for a single project.

Most granting agencies require the museum to submit a report describing how the grant was spent. The Grants Officer must keep these records up to date and complete. He or she must also monitor requests for payment from the granting agency once the grant has been received.

In addition the Grants Officer may:

- participate in informational meetings held by funding agencies
- assist the director of development in running special fund-raising campaigns
- provide secretarial support for the director of development

Salaries

Depending upon experience and responsibility, the Grants Officer makes between $15,000 and $22,000.

Employment Prospects

The Grants Officer can be an entry-level position in the museum which combines exposure to all departments of the organization with good administrative experience. Prospects are best in a small museum where the Grants Officer is a crucial member of the fund-raising team.

Advancement Prospects

Advancement prospects for the Grants Officer are quite good, especially since the position is a key liaison between the development, financial and curatorial departments. Inevitably activity will go beyond the processing of grants into other aspects of fund-raising, thus preparing the Grants Officer to become a director of development. As in all fund-raising jobs, success is measured by dollars earned, so a person in this position who creatively matches programs with appropriate funding sources will be greatly valued. Often the Grants Officer in a museum can advance to a position in a government or corporate funding agency.

Education

A degree in arts administration is desirable but not essential for this position. Coursework in art history, especially in the areas covered by the museum, is important, as are excellent writing skills. Secretarial training and proficiency on a word processor are valuable qualifications.

Experience and Skills

Familiarity with the procedures of government grants or in foundation administration is invaluable for a Grants Officer. He or she must be skilled in analyzing complex instructions and guidelines and in answering questions precisely and in clear, pithy prose. It is absolutely necessary that the Grants Officer be sensitive to the artistic goals and programs of the museum and be able to articulate them concisely and persuasively. Organizational skills are crucial in this job, which often calls upon the Grants Officer to process several different grants at once. He or she must be able to develop systems for processing information quickly and accurately in order to meet deadlines, and must also maintain files of the museum's fund-raising activity. A basic knowledge of accounting and the budget-making process is necessary.

DIRECTOR OF DEVELOPMENT

CAREER PROFILE

Duties: Plan and implement the museum's fund-raising strategy

Alternate Titles: Development Officer, Assistant Director for Fund-raising

Salary Range: $20,000 to $80,000

Employment Prospects: Fair

Advancement Prospects: Fair to good

Prerequisites:

Education—Undergraduate degree in business, arts administration or marketing

Experience—Extensive background in all areas of fund-raising

Special Skills—Excellent social skills, good writing ability and knowledge of art history

CAREER LADDER

```
┌─────────────────────────────┐
│                             │
│          Director           │
│                             │
└─────────────────────────────┘

┌─────────────────────────────┐
│                             │
│   Director of Development   │
│                             │
└─────────────────────────────┘

┌─────────────────────────────┐
│                             │
│       Grants Officer        │
│                             │
└─────────────────────────────┘
```

Position Description

As in all nonprofit organizations, fund-raising is crucial to a museum's financial health. The Director of Development, who is in charge of raising money from government, private and corporate sources, designs and implements fund-raising strategy. This job involves a great deal of pressure since, no matter how well-planned or intelligent his or her efforts are, the Director of Development cannot be sure they will meet with success. Regardless of the hit-or-miss quality of the job, development professionals are primarily evaluated on their performance, and an organization depends on their bringing in a certain percentage of the annual budget's funding.

In most museums the Director of Development supervises a grants officer, who prepares proposals to government agencies, foundations and corporations, and a membership officer, who works with auxiliary support groups and the general museum membership. While much of the day-to-day business of fund-raising is handled by these members of the department, the Director of Development is often out on the road meeting with the administrators of corporations and foundations and high-level individual supporters of the museum. It is more often through direct lobbying rather than letters and written proposals that the museum wins new benefactors. The Director of Development must blend a knowledge of museum programs with a persuasive, appealing social presentation.

In addition to this ongoing activity, the Director of Development plans and launches special fund-raising projects, like membership drives, endowment or building appeals and special benefits. To implement a fund-raising campaign the Director of Development works with key members of the museum's board of trustees to set goals and a strategy for appealing to donors.

Directors of Development must be creative, hardworking and tough-skinned professionals. They must understand the sometimes unreasonable demands made on them from within the museum's staff to raise money, and must compete with other arts organizations for limited private and public funds.

In addition, the Director of Development may:

- supervise earned income or marketing efforts
- assist in developing the annual budget
- prepare the museum's annual report
- coordinate activities of the board of trustees

Salaries

Since Directors of Development raise money, they are usually among the best-paid museum professionals. Although a Director of Development can make as little as $20,000 in a small museum, most make more and, depending on the size of the organization, average a salary in the 30s or 40s. Some Directors of Development make as much as $80,000.

Employment Prospects

Because of the pressure involved as well as the ever-present possibility that a Director of Development will not raise his or her portion of the operating budget, there is a reasonable amount of turnover in fund-raising positions. However, fund-raising, which includes a great deal of socializing and contact with the wealthy, is for many a glamorous and appealing job. So even though opportunities may open up frequently, competition is tough. Since fund-raising is both crucial to museum operations and difficult to guarantee, a professional with a proven track record has a great advantage.

Advancement Prospects

Since the Director of Development is the head of a department, his or her primary path of advancement within the museum is to director of finance, if this is a superior position, or director. It is unlikely, however, that one could advance to the position of director without considerable expertise in the artistic areas of the museum. A fund-raising professional with a proven track record has a very good chance of moving into a position with more responsibility at another museum or arts organization.

Education

A degree in business, arts administration, public relations or marketing is preferred, although a background in art history is also suitable. Coursework in writing and public speaking will come in handy.

Experience and Skills

As much as knowing how to look for money, the Director of Development must know where to look. This means an awareness of corporate, government and foundation sources which are appropriate to his or her organization, as well as the research skills to find new potential benefactors. Fund-raising professionals must be skilled in creating a network of colleagues and potential funders. Although the ability to adapt to virtually any social situation is a crucial skill, the Director of Development must also be able to understand and communicate the programs and goals of the museum, both verbally and in written form. On a practical level, he or she must be able to organize, implement and supervise an effective fund-raising campaign, know how government and foundation grants are processed and evaluated and be aware of the legal circumstances and tax benefits of individual giving.

DIRECTOR OF FINANCE

CAREER PROFILE

Duties: Responsibility for the museum's financial and personnel management policies and accounting procedures

Alternate Titles: Business Manager, Administrator

Salary Range: $15,000 to $70,000

Employment Prospects: Fair to good

Advancement Prospects: Fair

Prerequisites:

Education—Undergraduate degree in business or museum management; advanced degree preferred

Experience—Background in accounting, budget making and management, personnel management

Special Skills—Creativity in financial management, sensitivity to the special financial issues related to nonprofit organizations

CAREER LADDER

```
┌─────────────────────────────┐
│                             │
│          Director           │
│                             │
└─────────────────────────────┘

┌─────────────────────────────┐
│                             │
│     Director of Finance      │
│                             │
└─────────────────────────────┘

┌─────────────────────────────┐
│      Accountant or          │
│    Personnel Manager        │
│                             │
└─────────────────────────────┘
```

Position Description

The Director of Finance is responsible for the museum's financial management. He or she typically develops an annual budget, supervises personnel and operation of the physical plant, handles legal issues and maintains accounting procedures. Although the Director of Finance reports to the director, the position is often the top administrative post in a museum.

Since most museums receive a significant part of their income from foundations and public grants, the Director of Finance must be familiar with fund accounting and grants administration. Typically he or she works closely with the curatorial or development staff to prepare funding requests, and therefore must be aware of exhibition planning and collection management. Often the Director of Finance is also involved in maximizing the museum's earned income through store sales, food services or direct mail marketing.

In a large museum the Director of Finance can supervise hundreds of employees; even in a small institution, he or she must design and implement personnel policies, including salary guidelines, job descriptions and benefit packages. The Director of Finance must

oversee the maintenance and improvement of the museum building, including developing a plan for gallery guards and security as well as an insurance policy to cover collections, exhibited art and the physical plant.

Managing the finances of a museum is a creative job which inevitably requires flexibility and a talent for compromise. The annual budget is an important planning tool for all departments and its preparation requires sensitivity to artistic as well as financial priorities. Most nonprofit organizations have at least occasional cash flow difficulties, and the Director of Finance must establish procedures to accommodate unpredictable situations.

In addition the Director of Finance may:
- hire and fire administrative personnel
- participate in planning and fund-raising for an endowment
- plan and automate office procedures including computer and telephone systems

Salaries

The Director of Finance is typically one of the best-paid employees in a museum. In a large institution, he or she can make as much as $70,000, although a small museum may pay as little as $15,000. Since Directors of Finance have skills that are transferable outside of the nonprofit world, their salaries must be competitive with analogous posts in business.

Employment Prospects

Museums desperately need creative financial managers who are willing to take on the challenges the nonprofit world presents. With training in business and a strong interest in working in the arts, prospects are good. It is easier to begin in a smaller institution where responsibilities might include fund-raising and clerical work as well as financial planning. Organizational skills and a knowledge of accounting are crucial.

Advancement Prospects

The Director of Finance is in charge of one aspect of the museum's activity, so there is nowhere to advance within his or her department. It is possible to go on to the position of director, but this is unlikely unless the Director of Finance has considerable knowledge of art history and curatorial work. Chances are very good for a Director of Finance to advance to a better position in another museum or arts funding agency.

Education

An undergraduate degree in business or museum management is necessary, and an advanced degree in these fields is an advantage.

Experience and Skills

Since the budget is an important planning and administrative tool for the museum, the Director of Finance must be able to synthesize a complex set of needs and programs, drawing on many members of the museum's staff. He or she must be exceptionally creative in the approach to financial management and an adept manager of personnel. Although knowledge of accounting procedures is of primary importance, a sensitivity to art history and to the larger mission of the museum is invaluable.

DIRECTOR

CAREER PROFILE

Duties: Provide artistic, fund-raising and financial direction for the museum, and represent its programs to the institution's board of trustees and the public

Alternate Title: Executive Director

Salary Range: $42,000 to $120,000

Employment Prospects: Poor

Advancement Prospects: Good

Prerequisites:

Education—Undergraduate and advanced degrees in art history

Experience—Extensive work experience in museums and demonstrated curatorial and fund-raising ability

Special Skills—Leadership ability; excellent planning skills, speaking skills and interpersonal skills

CAREER LADDER

```
┌─────────────────────────────┐
│                             │
│          Director           │
│                             │
└─────────────────────────────┘

┌─────────────────────────────┐
│                             │
│        Chief Curator        │
│                             │
└─────────────────────────────┘

┌─────────────────────────────┐
│                             │
│          Curator            │
│                             │
└─────────────────────────────┘
```

Position Description

The Director of a museum gives conceptual form to its programs and collections. In doing so, he or she mediates between the governing body of the institution, or board of trustees, and the staff which implements programs. The Director must be adept at guiding museum trustees in their policymaking by representing his or her own attitudes and those of the staff. He or she must also be capable of leading museum employees to develop programs which meet the goals of the board of trustees in the areas of curatorial work, fund-raising and financial management.

Depending on the size of the museum, and the structure of its financial department, the Director plays an important role in maintaining financial stability. This usually means a good deal of fund-raising within the community. With the director of development, the Director courts corporations, individuals and government agencies to ensure required funding. As the most visible representative of the museum, the Director must be able to convey the goals of his or her organization to the community and the media. This includes a good deal of social activity as well as conversations with the press and, depending upon the size of the

museum and its stature, local and regional government officials.

The Director usually has a distinguished expertise in one of the areas of specialization of the museum. In addition to his or her financial and policy responsibilities, the Director helps negotiate major curatorial projects, like international exchanges, the acquisition of major works of art, or gifts from important art collectors. He or she may also undertake the organization of exhibitions or other curatorial projects.

The balance of these broad responsibilities varies significantly from museum to museum, depending upon how the staff is structured and what the interests of the Director are. In some cases, he or she may leave daily operations and program issues largely in the hands of his or her staff in order to pursue major long-range goals for the museum, such as the expansion of the building or the creation of new areas of specialization.

As the leader of the museum, the Director must supervise all personnel issues, including hiring, firing, creating new positions, and structuring benefit plans for employees. Administrative duties are compounded by the necessity of keeping up to date with the plans and projects of key staff members and dealing with personnel-related issues of morale and employee incentives. Especially in a small museum, the health of the organization rests largely on the creativity, strength and administrative know-how of the Director.

In addition the Director may:
- write an annual report for the museum
- take on honorary or advisory positions related to the museum's work in the community
- act as chief curator, especially in a small museum

Salaries

The average salary for a museum Director ranges from $42,000 to $50,000. As with most museum positions, however, salary is proportional to the size of the institution and can be as high as $120,000.

Employment Prospects

The position of Director is probably the most competitive post to attain in an extremely competitive field. Not only must a potential Director have distinguished him- or herself in an area of specialization covered by the museum, but he or she must also demonstrate an excellent track record for financial management and fund-raising. In most museums it is desirable for the Director to have charismatic appeal as well, and to have demonstrated effective policymaking. The choice of a Director for a particular institution largely depends on the long-range goals of that institution. For instance, if the museum is planning an expanded building, then it is likely that a Director will be hired who has already ushered a museum through such a phase of expansion. In a small museum a distinguished record as a chief curator may qualify a potential Director, but in many cases Directors are chosen from those who have already held the position in a similar institution.

Advancement Prospects

Once one has become a Director chances are reasonably good that he or she can gain a more prestigious directorship elsewhere. As with all museum work, however, a good reputation is crucial to advancement, and the Director must be distinguished in the areas of curatorial work, fund-raising and financial management. It is also possible that a museum Director would enter a related field: for instance, become the Director of a state funding agency or other arts policymaking body.

Education

In virtually every case it is necessary for the Director to have an advanced degree in an area of the museum's specialization. Coursework in museum management and administration issues is desirable. Training in writing and communications is particularly helpful.

Experience and Skills

The museum Director must combine a persuasive, charismatic personality with excellent knowledge of art history in his or her field and superior management and financial abilities. This is a rare combination, so it is especially important that the Director know his or her strengths and be able to structure a staff which takes full advantage of them and compensates for his or her weaknesses. The Director must have a specialized knowledge of at least one area of the museum's collections, or in the management of a particular type of museum. He or she must have the ability to implement the policy established by the museum's governing body, and must encourage active participation—both financial and conceptual—from the board of trustees. He or she must be able to communicate long-range policy to the staff as well as to the community. A good working knowledge of both the budgetmaking process and the particular fiscal characteristics of nonprofit organizations is absolutely necessary, as is familiarity with the legal aspects of museum operation and with current and prospective legislation affecting museums.

SECTION 3
ART GALLERIES

PREPARATOR

CAREER PROFILE

Duties: Prepare gallery for new shows; install exhibitions

Alternate Titles: None

Salary Range: $15,000 to $30,000

Employment Prospects: Fair

Advancement Prospects: Fair

Prerequisites:
  Education—Bachelor's degree preferred; carpentry training
  Experience—Art-handling experience required
  Special Skills—Carpentry; problem-solving skills

CAREER LADDER

```
┌──────────────────────────┐
│                          │
│         Registrar        │
│                          │
└──────────────────────────┘

┌──────────────────────────┐
│                          │
│         Preparator       │
│                          │
└──────────────────────────┘

┌──────────────────────────┐
│                          │
│          Intern          │
│                          │
└──────────────────────────┘
```

Position Description

The Preparator is responsible for readying the gallery for new exhibitions and installing the artwork for those exhibitions. The Preparator may be called upon to construct walls or pedestals, alter lighting, paint, and crate and uncrate artwork.

It is important for the Preparator to know how to handle art properly. The safe unpacking, display and repacking of artwork is done under the care of the Preparator.

The exhibit design is usually undertaken by the gallery owner or director; the Preparator carries out their instructions, sometimes with the help of a crew of temporary workers. Long hours must be logged before an opening. The Preparator should be well organized and able to work under deadline pressure.

Salaries

The Preparator can earn from $15,000 to $30,000 a year, depending on his or her skills and on the gallery's size and location.

Employment Prospects

Chances for employment as a Preparator are fair. Competition is somewhat less intense for this position than for other gallery jobs because of the special skillls required.

Advancement Prospects

The Preparator has a fair chance of advancing if he or she can gain some experience as a registrar. This would most commonly be done by making a lateral move into the registrar's position in a gallery.

Education

Preparators usually have bachelor's degrees, along with some kind of apprenticeship with a carpenter.

Experience and Skills

Previous gallery or museum experience is necessary to gain skill in the proper handling of artwork. Carpentry is the most important skill for a Preparator. He or she should also be a good problem solver and an organized person.

Organizations and Associations

Gallery employees may wish to join one of the many art dealers' associations (see Appendix IV).

Tips for Entry

Those interested in becoming Preparators should look for part-time or volunteer work on installation crews in museums or art galleries.

ARCHIVIST

CAREER PROFILE

Duties: Prepare artist biographies; assemble bibliographies; handle curator relations; maintain photographic files of artwork

Alternate Title: Researcher

Salary Range: $12,000 to $25,000

Employment Prospects: Fair

Advancement Prospects: Fair

Prerequisites:

Education—Bachelor's degree required; art history background preferred

Experience—Previous work in a gallery or museum

Special Skills—Research and writing skills; organizational skills

CAREER LADDER

```
┌─────────────────────────────┐
│                             │
│         Registrar           │
│                             │
└─────────────────────────────┘

┌─────────────────────────────┐
│                             │
│         Archivist           │
│                             │
└─────────────────────────────┘

┌─────────────────────────────┐
│                             │
│   Receptionist or Student   │
│                             │
└─────────────────────────────┘
```

Position Description

The Archivist handles many of the documentation functions of the gallery. He or she must research and keep files on the provenance of the gallery's artwork and must prepare biographies of the artists represented. The Archivist also works up bibliographies relating to works in the gallery. He or she maintains photo documentation files of the artwork.

The Archivist usually takes care of the gallery's relations with museum curators, who may request loans of artwork in the gallery's possession. In addition, the Archivist helps to prepare catalogues for gallery exhibitions.

In smaller galleries the Archivist's functions may be handled by the registrar.

Salaries

Compensation for Archivists ranges from $12,000 to $25,000 per year, depending on gallery size and location.

Employment Prospects

The chances of finding a job as an Archivist are fair.

There are relatively few such positions available, but the turnover in them is reasonably rapid.

Advancement Prospects

The Archivist has a fair chance of being promoted to another position within a gallery. Generally speaking, the Archivist can expect to spend some time working as a registrar before moving up to the job of gallery director.

Education

The Archivist should have a bachelor's degree, preferably with a major in art or art history.

Experience and Skills

Previous experience in an art gallery or museum is required of the prospective Archivist. The Archivist must have strong research and writing abilities. In addition, he or she should have excellent organizational skills for the recordkeeping aspects of the job.

Organizations and Associations

Archivists might wish to join one of the art dealers' organizations listed in Appendix IV.

BUSINESS MANAGER

CAREER PROFILE

Duties: Handle bookkeeping, payroll, payables and receivables; order supplies

Alternate Title: Office Manager

Salary Range: $15,000 to $30,000

Employment Prospects: Fair

Advancement Prospects: Fair

Prerequisites:

Education—Bachelor's degree; accounting and business courses required

Experience—Bookkeeping

Special Skills—Detail orientation; organizational skills

CAREER LADDER

```
┌─────────────────────────────┐
│                             │
│      Gallery Director        │
│                             │
└─────────────────────────────┘

┌─────────────────────────────┐
│                             │
│      Business Manager        │
│                             │
└─────────────────────────────┘

┌─────────────────────────────┐
│                             │
│    Registrar or Accountant   │
│                             │
└─────────────────────────────┘
```

Position Description

The Business Manager of an art gallery is responsible for the smooth running of the gallery's accounts. He or she handles the bookkeeping, including payroll, accounts receivable and accounts payable. The Business Manager usually does the purchasing of supplies, setting up a purchase order system.

Though the Business Manager has little direct involvement with customers and artists, he or she may assist clients on the telephone. The position offers good preparation for an individual who hopes eventually to become a gallery owner.

Salaries

The Business Manager can expect to make between $15,000 and $30,000, depending on the size and geographic location of the gallery and on his or her own level of expertise.

Employment Prospects

An individual with some gallery experience and some business background has a fair chance of finding a job as a Business Manager.

Advancement Prospects

Chances for advancement are fair. The Business Manager may find a position as a gallery director if he or she has a good deal of experience. Alternatively, the Manager could move into a registrar or archivist position in order to gain additional experience.

Education

The Business Manager should have a bachelor's degree with some background in both art and business. Any accounting coursework will be especially useful.

Experience and Skills

Bookkeeping experience is required of an aspiring Business Manager. Because the Business Manager is responsible for the business aspects of the gallery, he or she should be a well-organized, detail-oriented person.

Organizations and Associations

Gallery employees may wish to join one of the art dealers' organizations (see Appendix IV).

REGISTRAR

CAREER PROFILE

Duties: Recordkeeping; tracking of artwork; appraising condition of pieces; complete familiarity with collection

Alternate Titles: None

Salary Range: $15,000 to $40,000

Employment Prospects: Fair

Advancement Prospects: Good

Prerequisites:

   Education—Bachelor's degree required; art history major preferred

   Experience—Previous gallery or museum work

   Special Skills—Administrative and organizational ability

CAREER LADDER

```
+---------------------------+
|                           |
|      Gallery Director      |
|                           |
+---------------------------+

+---------------------------+
|                           |
|        Registrar           |
|                           |
+---------------------------+

+---------------------------+
|                           |
|        Archivist           |
|                           |
+---------------------------+
```

Position Description

The Registrar is responsible for the tracking and maintenance of all artwork held by the gallery. This includes extensive recordkeeping relating to the works, their condition, and their history; tracking of the exact location of works as they move between warehouse and gallery and out on loan for exhibition; proper packing, transportation, and unpacking of works; and insurance of such pieces.

In addition, the Registrar may be involved in assisting customers, handling unsolicited materials from artists who wish to work with the gallery, or such archivist duties as catalogue preparation and research on specific pieces.

The Registrar must be completely familiar with all the gallery's holdings. The position of Registrar is a pivotal one within the gallery, as most higher positions are available only to persons who have strong Registrar experience.

Salaries

The Registrar can expect to make between $15,000 and $40,000 a year. Naturally, the higher salaries go to experienced Registrars in major art galleries.

Employment Prospects

The chances of finding a job as a Registrar are fair. Because Registrar experience is vital to people interested in both gallery and museum careers, the competition can be intense.

Advancement Prospects

An experienced Registrar has a good chance of advancing in his or her career. Having gained valuable Registrar experience, he or she becomes qualified for the position of gallery director or of Registrar at a larger gallery.

Education

A bachelor's degree, preferably in art history, is required by most galleries.

Experience and Skills

The aspiring Registrar should have some previous experience working in a museum or art gallery. It is important for the Registrar to have excellent administration skills. The Registrar oversees a large number of files that must be kept current and well organized.

Organizations and Associations

Gallery employees may join one or more of the art dealers' organizations (see Appendix IV).

Tips for Entry

Because previous experience is so important for a Registrar, the job candidate should consider part-time or volunteer work at a gallery or museum. Secretarial or work-crew experience will be a plus on the resume, and the contacts made can be valuable.

GALLERY DIRECTOR

CAREER PROFILE

Duties: Manage gallery; assist customers; make sales; handle publicity; help plan shows

Alternate Titles: None

Salary Range: $20,000 to $60,000

Employment Prospects: Fair

Advancement Prospects: Poor

Prerequisites:

Education—Bachelor's degree required; art background preferred

Experience—Previous work as a registrar

Special Skills—Interpersonal skills; sales ability; art knowledge

CAREER LADDER

```
┌─────────────────────────────┐
│                             │
│      Gallery Owner          │
│                             │
└─────────────────────────────┘

┌─────────────────────────────┐
│                             │
│      Gallery Director       │
│                             │
└─────────────────────────────┘

┌─────────────────────────────┐
│                             │
│        Registrar            │
│                             │
└─────────────────────────────┘
```

Position Description

The Gallery Director is hired by the gallery owner to handle the day-to-day operations of the gallery. The owner determines the direction of the gallery, choosing artists and setting the themes for shows; the Director carries out the owner's wishes in preparing and presenting the shows.

The Director works with customers, assisting them and making sales. He or she must be familiar with the artwork inventory of the gallery and knowledgeable about the artists represented.

The Director usually handles publicity, mainly in the form of press releases regarding the openings of new exhibitions. He or she also manages the other employees of the gallery and deals with the gallery's artists in the owner's absence.

Because the preparation of a show can be hectic, the Director often works evenings and weekends.

Salaries

Salaries for Gallery Directors vary widely according to gallery size, geographic location and an individual's experience. The range of salaries is roughly from $20,000 to $60,000 per year.

Employment Prospects

Chances for employment as a Gallery Director are fair. Major cities have many galleries, and an individual with solid gallery experience should be able to find a Director's job.

Advancement Prospects

There is little opportunity to advance from the position of Gallery Director unless one has the capital to open a gallery of his or her own.

Education

Most Gallery Directors have bachelor's degrees. The usual majors are art and art history, but requirements are generally not strict; any liberal arts background is acceptable.

Experience and Skills

A Gallery Director should have several years' experience in gallery work, particularly as a registrar. Sales ability is important to a Director. He or she should also have strong interpersonal skills in order to deal effectively with customers, employees and artists.

Organizations and Associations

Gallery employees might join any of the gallery associations (see Appendix IV).

SECTION 4
EDUCATION

ART TEACHER

CAREER PROFILE

Duties: Instruct students in studio art techniques; grade student artwork; advise students

Alternate Title: Studio Art Instructor

Salary Range: $10,000 to $30,000

Employment Prospects: Fair

Advancement Prospects: Poor

Prerequisites:

Education—Bachelor of fine arts degree usually required; master of fine arts degree preferred; teaching certificate may be required

Experience—Work as an artist

Special Skills—Teaching ability; communications ability

CAREER LADDER

```
┌─────────────────────────────────┐
│   Art Department Chairperson     │
│               or                 │
│      Art School Director         │
└─────────────────────────────────┘

┌─────────────────────────────────┐
│                                  │
│          Art Teacher             │
│                                  │
└─────────────────────────────────┘

┌─────────────────────────────────┐
│                                  │
│       Student or Artist          │
│                                  │
└─────────────────────────────────┘
```

Position Description

An Art Teacher instructs students in various art skills. Art Teachers work on many levels—in elementary and secondary schools, in colleges and art schools, in adult and community education programs, and with private students. Art Teachers may also specialize in terms of the media they teach. For instance, an elementary school Art Teacher is likely to help students work in painting, drawing, and clay modeling, but an art school Instructor will probably specialize in oil painting or metal sculpture or pastels.

Clearly, the environments in which Art Teachers work vary widely, and the prospective Teacher should do some thinking about the kind of environment he or she prefers. Elementary and secondary school Art Teachers work with young people, helping them to enjoy art, while looking for early signs of talent. Such Teachers must have college degrees and teaching certification, including several education courses and student teaching experience.

College Art Instructors work with more advanced students. Generally, such Instructors will have earned master of fine arts degrees. They tend to specialize in one medium, and they instruct students in art theory and practice. As college Instructors, they may move up and become assistant, associate and full professors.

Art school Teachers may not have any particular educational background, but they will have experience in working as artists. In a community art school, the Teachers may be local art hobbyists, but in a studio art conservatory the Teachers would be accomplished and recognized in their fields.

Of course, an important part of teaching art students is the evaluation and constructive criticism of their work. The Teacher is there to help the student to improve his or her skills and to advise the student regarding future work. In addition, the Art Teacher may be involved with curriculum planning for the art department.

Salaries

Because the positions themselves vary greatly, there is a wide range of salaries—from $10,000 to $30,000 per year. Part-time Teachers would earn proportionally less. The highest salaries are offered on the college and professional art school level.

Employment Prospects

It is somewhat difficult to find a position as an Art Teacher. Many art graduates look to teaching as a way to supplement the income from their own artwork, or as a way to make a living until they can afford to become full-time artists. Consequently, the competition is keen.

Advancement Prospects

Advancement in this career is difficult to achieve. There is great competition for promotion on the college level. In other areas of art teaching, the only avenue for advancement is to move up to administration, and there are only a few administrative positions available.

Education

As noted above, educational requirements vary according to the type of school in which one wishes to teach, with colleges requiring master's degrees, elementary and high schools requiring bachelor's degrees and teaching certificates, and other schools basing their requirements upon experience.

Art Teachers should be able to communicate well with their students and to criticize their work in a helpful and constructive way. Of course, they should also have strong art skills of their own.

Organizations and Associations

The major organization for Art Teachers is the National Art Education Association (see Appendix IV).

Tips for Entry

Those seeking to enter this field might gain experience by teaching art to children at a camp or in an after-school program, either in a paid position or as a volunteer.

ART SCHOOL DIRECTOR

CAREER PROFILE

Duties: Managing business aspects of school; teaching art; hiring, marketing, scheduling

Alternate Title: Art School Dean

Salary Range: $10,000 to $40,000

Employment Prospects: Poor

Advancement Prospects: Poor

Prerequisites:

Education—Bachelor's degree in art or art education

Experience—Teaching art in public or private school

Special Skills—Art skills, teaching skills, business acumen, ability to deal with the public

CAREER LADDER

```
┌─────────────────────────────┐
│                             │
│     Art School Director     │
│                             │
└─────────────────────────────┘

┌─────────────────────────────┐
│                             │
│         Art Teacher         │
│                             │
└─────────────────────────────┘

┌─────────────────────────────┐
│                             │
│     Student or Artist       │
│                             │
└─────────────────────────────┘
```

Position Description

An Art School Director manages—and, often, owns—a private art school. Such a school is generally small and geared to providing enrichment to school-age youngsters. It may also cater to senior citizens and others pursuing art as a hobby, but only a few such schools offer professional-level training to people who are planning careers as artists.

The School Director is responsible for the smooth functioning of the school, including both its business and instructional aspects. The Director must arrange for classroom space, teaching personnel and materials to work with. The Director recruits students through advertising, personal contacts, open houses and the like. He or she must see to general office functions, such as bookkeeping and correspondence, and handle class scheduling.

The Director is assumed to be knowledgeable about art education, and he or she will supervise and perhaps train the school's teachers. The Director may teach classes as well.

Many Art School Directors own their schools, so they are entrepreneurs who may see this as their ultimate goal. Others are employed as directors, and they may go on to larger schools, to careers as working artists, or to become owners of their own art schools.

Salaries

An Art School Director may make from $10,000 per year in a small school to approximately $40,000 in a larger school. A self-employed owner/director may make more than this if his or her school is especially profitable.

Employment Prospects

The opportunities to become an Art School Director are poor unless one has the capital to start one's own school. There are many art educators who are qualified to handle the educational aspects of the position, but a business background will greatly enhance an art teacher's qualifications for this job.

Advancement Prospects

Advancement from this position is unlikely. Only rarely will an Art School Director move up to head a larger or more prestigious school. An owner/director may consider greater profitability to be a kind of advancement.

Education

Most Art School Directors have at least bachelor's degrees in art education. Many have master's degrees in art education, and a number of practical business courses would be extremely helpful.

Experience and Skills

The Director should have several years' experience as an art teacher. Any experience in business and in dealing with the public will be useful. Demonstrated success as a working artist may help the Director to attract students to the school.

In addition to art and teaching skills, the Art School Director should have some sales and marketing ability, managerial skills, and good communication skills (in order to recruit students for the school).

Organizations and Associations

An Art School Director may be a member of the National Art Education Association (see Appendix IV).

Tips for Entry

The candidate for this job should be articulate. Public relations is an important aspect of the position; an introverted "artist type" will find it difficult to succeed.

ART HISTORY INSTRUCTOR

CAREER PROFILE

Duties: Teach art history on the college level; advise students; work on curriculum; research and write on art history

Alternate Titles: Art History Teacher, Art History Professor

Salary Range: $15,000 to $35,000

Employment Prospects: Fair

Advancement Prospects: Poor

Prerequisites:

Education—Master's degree in art history required; doctorate preferred

Experience—Teaching

Special Skills—Research and writing skills; communications skills

CAREER LADDER

```
┌─────────────────────────────┐
│  Art History Deparment      │
│  Chairperson                │
└─────────────────────────────┘

┌─────────────────────────────┐
│                             │
│  Art History Instructor     │
│                             │
└─────────────────────────────┘

┌─────────────────────────────┐
│                             │
│  Student                    │
│                             │
└─────────────────────────────┘
```

Position Description

An Art History Instructor educates college students on art history. A beginning Instructor may give a survey course covering a wide portion of the history of art; as the Instructor gains experience, he or she is more likely to give more specialized courses on particular periods, movements, artists or media.

The Art History Instructor may be hired strictly on a courses-taught basis, being paid by the credit (this is often the case in community colleges), or may be hired onto a "tenure track," with the hope of progressing to assistant, associate and, finally, full professor of art history. Tenure track Instructors must devote considerable time to independent research and writing in art history, as the publication of articles and books is important to their career advancement.

All Art History Instructors spend time preparing lectures, grading papers, advising students, and performing whatever paperwork the university requires of them.

Salaries

Art History Instructors generally make $15,000 to $35,000 per year, with the higher salaries going to the more experienced Instructors. Part-time teaching work may be available for those interested in the field; such work is usually compensated by a flat fee per course or credit taught.

Employment Prospects

It is difficult to find a position as an Art History Instructor. There are more graduates in this field than there are positions available, so the competition for jobs is keen.

Advancement Prospects

Advancement opportunities are very limited in this field. In a community college, an experienced and accomplished Instructor may move up to become chairperson of the art history department, but in a university the Instructors must produce publications of high quality—as well as perform their normal classroom duties—in order to achieve promotion.

Education

Art History Instructors must have master's degrees in their field, and the doctoral degree is required for most positions.

Experience and Skills

Teaching experience, usually gained while a graduate student, is required for this position. The Instructor should have excellent communications and teaching skills. Research and writing ability are important to those hoping to advance in their careers.

Organizations and Associations

The National Art Education Association is the organization for this profession (see Appendix IV).

Tips for Entry

In order to find a teaching job, the graduate student should work to make contacts with art history professors at many colleges. Publication of articles in art history will help the graduate student to become known in the field.

ART THERAPIST

CAREER PROFILE

Duties: Diagnose and treat clients using art therapy techniques

Alternate Titles: None

Salary Range: $10,000 to $35,000

Employment Prospects: Fair

Advancement Prospects: Poor

Prerequisites:
Education—Bachelor's degree required; master's preferred

Experience—Apprenticeship as part of educational program

Special Skills—Sensitivity, communications skills, art skills

CAREER LADDER

```
┌─────────────────────────┐
│                         │
│        Supervisor       │
│                         │
└─────────────────────────┘

┌─────────────────────────┐
│                         │
│       Art Therapist     │
│                         │
└─────────────────────────┘

┌─────────────────────────┐
│                         │
│         Student         │
│                         │
└─────────────────────────┘
```

Position Description

Art therapy is a helping profession in which psychological and creative arts skills are used to diagnose and treat emotional problems or to foster self-awareness and personal growth. Art Therapists are trained to work with people in such settings as nursing homes, hospitals, schools, guidance centers and private practices.

Art Therapists are trained in both art and psychotherapy, and any of a variety of psychological approaches may be applied to art therapy. But the underlying principle of art therapy is that there are emotional benefits available through the use of art media to express and communicate feelings.

An Art Therapist may work alone in a private practice or may function in an institutional setting, but increasingly Art Therapists are found working as members of therapeutic teams. Such teams may include psychologists, psychiatrists, nurses, occupational therapists, social workers and others who work together to help clients or patients. Clients may be treated individually or in groups.

Salaries

Salaries for Art Therapists range from about $10,000 per year to about $35,000 per year. Those who work in larger institutions and those who have more experience are likely to receive higher pay. Art Therapists in private practice earn amounts that vary according to the number of people they see in their practices.

Employment Prospects

Art Therapy is a relatively new and growing field, and there is an increasing number of positions available, especially for a graduate who can creatively develop new opportunities for the specialty. Thus a well-prepared Art Therapist has a fair chance of finding a position.

Advancement Prospects

Opportunities for advancement in the field of art therapy are limited. In larger institutions, an Art Therapist might be promoted to supervise other Art Therapists or a therapy team, but such positions are difficult to find. In general, the Therapist would continue to practice in that position.

Education

Training for art therapy is specialized and is offered at relatively few colleges. Undergraduate preparation at a college with a program accredited by the American Art Therapy Association is a must, and a master's degree is increasingly required for employment in the field.

Art therapy education includes study in the fine arts and the behavioral and social sciences. Specialized art therapy training includes study of the history, theory and practice of art therapy.

Experience and Skills

Art therapy students receive practical experience as part of their training, but any additional paid or volunteer work with children, older adults or emotionally troubled people will be beneficial.

An Art Therapist should have a compassionate nature and should be sensitive to others. Certainly a caring and understanding personality is needed in order to function well in this field. Art skills and creative ability are important, as is a positive, helpful attitude.

Organizations and Associations

The American Art Therapy Association is the main organization for Art Therapists (see Appendix IV). It is also possible that Art Therapists working in hospital or school settings might join an employees' union on site.

Tips for Entry

Any work with people—paid or volunteer—will be beneficial to those wishing to enter this field. All types of art experience—classes, independent work, museum-going—are helpful, too.

SECTION 5
FUNDING AGENCIES
FOR THE ARTS

INTERN

Duties: Provide clerical and research support for agency personnel

Salary Range: 0 to $10,000

Employment Prospects: Fair to good

Advancement Prospects: Fair to good

Prerequisites:

Education—Enrollment in undergraduate program in the arts or humanities

Experience—Secretarial and research ability

Special Skills—Self-motivation, good organizational ability, clerical and research skills

```
┌─────────────────────────────┐
│                             │
│  Assistant Program Specialist│
│                             │
└─────────────────────────────┘

┌─────────────────────────────┐
│                             │
│   Administrative Assistant  │
│                             │
└─────────────────────────────┘

┌─────────────────────────────┐
│                             │
│           Intern            │
│                             │
└─────────────────────────────┘
```

Position Description

Many funding agencies offer internships, sometimes with a stipend and sometimes on a volunteer basis. Regardless of payment, an internship is an excellent means to learn about the activities of a funding agency, and can help prepare the Intern for positions in a wide range of nonprofit fund-raising or foundation jobs. Usually Interns work within a particular funding program, and provide clerical, research or secretarial support for the staff of that program. Internships range in length from three months or a year to two or three years.

Interns usually help the administrative assistant for a program with his or her responsibilities. For instance, the Intern might be asked to log in grant applications received from the field, and check that they are complete. He or she may be asked to file these applications, or copy them for panelists who will judge them.

Funding decisions are made not by the staff of the funding agency itself, but by a panel of independent experts chosen by the funding agency. When these panelists are in town, the Intern may be expected to help them in any way necessary: take them to their hotels, arrange entertainment for them, or answer questions about the logistics of the panel meetings. The Intern may also help the administrative assistant to research possible panelists.

The Intern is expected to assist in typing, filing and other clerical duties of the department. He or she may be asked by the program specialist or assistant program specialist to work on a special project. For instance, if the funding agency is planning a new initiative, the intern may be asked to research similar programs in other funding agencies in the United States or around the world.

In addition the intern may:

• assist with bulk mailings
• keep a file of background materials such as books and magazines in appropriate areas of the arts

Salaries

Typically, internships carry a very limited stipend, if any at all. They may pay $1,000 for a summer's internship or $10,000 for the entire year, and sometimes more.

Employment Prospects

Serving an internship is a way in which to work for a funding agency without having any other experience than a college degree, or in some cases only a few years of college. Although extensive background is not necessary, the competition for internships can be tough, especially at a large federal funding agency. Applicants will need to have a distinguished academic record, with extracurricular activities that demonstrate an interest in the arts.

Advancement Prospects

Prospects for advancement vary depending upon the structure of the internship. In some cases, it is meant only as a form of training, and the likelihood of being hired is slight. In other internships, it is assumed that an Intern who performs well has a good chance of rising to the position of administrative assistant or assistant program specialist.

Education

An Intern should have an undergraduate degree or be enrolled in an undergraduate program in the arts or in administration.

Experience and Skills

The Intern must have excellent research and clerical skills, and should have excellent typing or word processing ability. Organizational skills, tact and the ability to work under pressure are necessary. In order to make the most of his or her experience, the Intern should be someone who can take the initiative and learn well from observation. Sometimes internships lack structure, and it is important that participants are able to ask for what they want to know or are able to find it out themselves by using the staff and facilities of the funding agency.

ADMINISTRATIVE ASSISTANT

CAREER PROFILE

Duties: Provide administrative support for a department or senior personnel

Alternate Title: Secretary

Salary Range: $12,000 to $30,000

Employment Prospects: Fair to good

Advancement Prospects: Poor to fair

Prerequisites:

Education—Secretarial school or undergraduate degree in the arts or a related field

Experience—Background in secretarial skills and administration

Special Skills—Excellent typing, word processing, filing and other clerical abilities; excellent organizational skills

CAREER LADDER

```
┌─────────────────────────────────┐
│   Assistant Program Specialist   │
└─────────────────────────────────┘

┌─────────────────────────────────┐
│    Administrative Assistant      │
└─────────────────────────────────┘

┌─────────────────────────────────┐
│       Intern or College          │
└─────────────────────────────────┘
```

Position Description

The Administrative Assistant is responsible to one person or department, and provides overall administrative support. In a program area he or she would set up all panel meetings, coordinate all written and verbal contact, and follow up with panelists and update files and payments to them. Responsiblities might also include computerizing a regularly updated panelist contact file that would contain relevant data about panelists' work, credibility in particular disciplines or art organizational talents, and other pertinent information.

An Administrative Assistant in the budget and management area of the agency would provide advanced technical and business support; maintain administrative procedures in the department or agency-wide; and suggest improvements in these procedures. He or she might be involved in processing routine requests for funds from granted artists or organizations, and assist in answering questions from the agency's constituency about financial policy.

Regardless of what area the Administrative Assistant serves in, he or she has extensive clerical and secretarial duties. There is a great deal of paperwork involved in government agencies, and the Administrative Assistant must be able to perform it efficiently and well. In the case of an Administrative Assistant in a program area, checking applications from outside artists or organizations for completeness is an important duty.

Although Administrative Assistants are primarily support staff, funding agencies, like most arts-related organizations, are often understaffed and someone in this position may be asked to take on some of the duties of the program specialist or assistant program specialist.

In addition the Administrative Assistant may:

* type all correspondence for a person or department
* coordinate the production of designed materials or information
* manage bulk mailings to the agency's constituency

Salaries

Salaries range from $12,000 to $30,000 depending on the size of the funding agency and the extent of responsibilities.

Employment Prospects

The Administrative Assistant is an entry-level position, so prospects are reasonably good that someone with basic secretarial or accounting training and with a demonstrated interest in the arts could obtain this position.

Advancement Prospects

Since this position is primarily secretarial, chances are not too good for advancement. If the funding agency is small, or very busy, and the Administrative Assistant is able to take on duties related to the conception and running of a program or other department, chances are better to advance.

Education

Secretarial school or basic training in accounting are necessary. But the applicant is also usually required to have a degree in the arts or a related field.

Experience and Skills

The Administrative Assistant must have excellent research, clerical and accounting skills. He or she must be proficient in using a computer either for word processing or to create financial spread sheets. The person who fills this job must be very organized, able to communicate well on the telephone and have adequate writing skills. Since Administrative Assistants often have to balance duties given to them by several members of a department, they must have a good sense of humor and be able to work under pressure.

ASSISTANT PROGRAM SPECIALIST

CAREER PROFILE

Duties: Assist program specialist in administration and management of an agency program

Salary Range: $15,000 to $30,000

Employment Prospects: Fair

Advancement Prospects: Good

Prerequisites:
Education—Undergraduate degree in the arts or humanities or in arts administration

Experience—Background in administration and management, preferably in the arts

Special Skills—Good organizational skills, attention to detail

CAREER LADDER

```
┌─────────────────────────────────────┐
│        Program Specialist            │
└─────────────────────────────────────┘

┌─────────────────────────────────────┐
│    Assistant Program Specialist      │
└─────────────────────────────────────┘

┌─────────────────────────────────────┐
│    Administrative Assistant or       │
│             College                  │
└─────────────────────────────────────┘
```

Position Description

The Assistant Program Specialist is primarily responsible for the day-to-day administration of a granting program. Under the supervision of the program specialist, he or she manages communications with constituents of the program, reviews applications from the field to be sure the applicants are eligible for the particular program, monitors budgets for grants which are given and generally assists the program specialist with all of his or her duties.

In order to make artists and art institutions aware of their programs, funding agencies publish their guidelines, complete with instructions and application forms. Not only does the Assistant Program Specialist assist in the preparation of these materials, but he or she must also ensure their effective distribution. This involves maintaining an accurate and comprehensive mailing list, and making periodic bulk mailings. Like the program specialist, the Assistant Program Specialist regularly speaks on the phone with constituents to discuss their plans and whether they are competitive for funding.

Most funding agencies require very specific sorts of written material and documentation with a grant application. When applications arrive, the Assistant Program Specialist must review them to be sure that all of this material is included. If elements are missing, he or she must call the applicant and request supplementary material. Once a grant is given, the funded organization—a museum, for instance—must request the funds with special forms, often including extensive documentation of money spent. The Assistant Program Specialist must maintain this system effectively and be sure that all requests for grant money are legitimate.

In a large program—for instance, the Museum Program at the National Endowment for the Arts—an Assistant Program Specialist may have primary responsibility for a subsection of the program, like Special Exhibitions or Catalogues.

In addition, the Assistant Program Specialist may:
- undertake research for the program specialist in order to find expert panelists in the field
- make travel or entertainment arrangements for expert panelists
- write and distribute press releases on the agency's funding program

Salaries

Salaries range between $15,000 and $30,000, and may be more in a large funding agency.

Employment Prospects

The Assistant Program Specialist could be an entry-level position for someone with education in the arts and good administrative skills. However, as with most positions in the arts, competition can be very difficult. In a situation where the Assistant Program Specialist has significant individual responsibility, experience in the arts is essential.

Advancement Prospects

The prospects are good that an Assistant Program Specialist will advance to the position of program specialist after a number of years in the job. Chances are better if he or she has taken primary responsibility for one sub-area of the funding program.

Education

A degree in the appropriate area of the arts or a related field is necessary. Special education in administration is also a plus. Any training in the use of computers or secretarial skills is also an advantage.

Experience and Skills

Anyone who works in a funding agency must be sensitive to following the procedures which it dictates. This is especially true for an Assistant Program Specialist, who must have both an excellent head for detail and efficient organization. Excellent communications skills are a must, as is a good knowledge of the area of the arts within which he or she will work. The ability to work with budgets is invaluable.

PROGRAM SPECIALIST

CAREER PROFILE

Duties: Manage a funding agency program

Salary Range: $20,000 to $50,000

Employment Prospects: Fair

Advancement Prospects: Good

Prerequisites:

   Education—Undergraduate degree in the arts or related field

   Experience—Background in arts administration, preferably in a government setting

   Special Skills—Expert knowledge of the arts in special field; ability to work with a constituency; political acumen; excellent writing and speaking skills

CAREER LADDER

```
┌─────────────────────────────────┐
│                                 │
│      Program Coordinator        │
│                                 │
└─────────────────────────────────┘

┌─────────────────────────────────┐
│                                 │
│      Program Specialist         │
│                                 │
└─────────────────────────────────┘

┌─────────────────────────────────┐
│                                 │
│   Assistant Program Specialist  │
│                                 │
└─────────────────────────────────┘
```

Position Description

Under supervision of the program coordinator, Program Specialists are responsible for the planning, management and representation of a particular granting program. In general, this includes regular contact with a constituency, administration of day-to-day operations for the program, working with staff in other departments as needed, and supervising tasks performed by the assistant program specialist. Responsibilities include administering the budget for this area, including monitoring current expenditures and anticipating future needs.

Most funding agencies try to tailor their programs to the needs which exist in the field. For that reason, the Program Specialist spends a good deal of time assessing needs and trends. He or she must evaluate the accomplishments of the program and propose changes to address its shortcomings. When new initiatives are proposed, the Program Specialist must assess the budget implications and constituency effectiveness of all changes. If, for instance, the Program Specialist manages a section of the funding agency which gives money to museum exhibitions, he or she will spend a good deal of time on the phone with museum curators, hearing about the projects they wish to propose and advising them how to apply successfully.

The decisions to give away money, however, are not made by the staff of the funding agency itself, but by a panel, which changes each year, of experts in the field. The Program Specialist must choose these panelists and organize their review and discussion of all proposals. Before these panels meet, the Program Specialist, often with the assistance of the assistant program specialist, must review applications to make sure they fit the funding agency's guidelines and include all of the information necessary.

Once funding decisions have been made the Program Specialist must notify all applicants, answering the questions of those who did not receive a grant, and explaining the terms of the gift to those who did. The Program Specialist supervises the disbursement of funds to grant recipients, and solicits final reports on all projects funded.

In addition, the Program Specialist may:

- assist organizations which need special help in writing grants
- recruit applications from the field
- communicate the goals of his or her program to other Program Specialists, and perhaps jointly plan special initiatives

Salaries

The average salary for a Program Specialist is between $20,000 and $52,000, largely depending upon the scale of the funding agency. Usually federal salaries are higher than those of state arts councils.

Employment Prospects

Since Program Specialists work directly with artistic projects, and often with artists, it is a desirable position, and is usually quite difficult to obtain. Experience in a museum or other art institution, as well as administrative expertise, is invaluable.

Advancement Prospects

Advancement prospects for Program Specialists are quite good. If they show talent in running their programs, they will have a good chance to advance to the position of assistant program coordinator or program coordinator.

Education

An undergraduate degree in the arts or in education or a related field is required, and a graduate degree in a similar field may be an advantage. Formal training in administration could also be a plus.

Experience and Skills

The Program Specialist must have experience in planning for and managing a major arts program, preferably with broad and varied experience in arts presentation. He or she must be able to identify needs, opportunities and trends that relate to the creation of art appropriate to their program. Since a great part of this job is communicating with an arts constituency, the Program Specialist's communication skills, as well as his or her written skills, must be outstanding. The ability to manage a budget effectively is necessary, as are efficiency and the ability to get along in a bureaucratic environment.

ASSISTANT PROGRAM COORDINATOR

CAREER PROFILE

Duties: Assist program coordinator in managing an agency department or cluster of programs

Alternate Title: Assistant Director of Department

Salary Range: $23,000 to $35,000

Employment Prospects: Fair to good

Advancement Prospects: Fair

Prerequisites:
   Education—Undergraduate degree in the arts or art administration

   Experience—Background in administration and management, preferably arts related

   Special Skills—Sensitivity to art; excellent organizational and management skills; writing and speaking ability

CAREER LADDER

```
┌─────────────────────────────────┐
│                                 │
│      Program Coordinator         │
│                                 │
└─────────────────────────────────┘

┌─────────────────────────────────┐
│                                 │
│   Assistant Program Coordinator  │
│                                 │
└─────────────────────────────────┘

┌─────────────────────────────────┐
│   Assistant Program Specialist   │
│                or                │
│             College              │
└─────────────────────────────────┘
```

Position Description

Whereas the program coordinator undertakes the program-related and budget planning for a particular department of the funding agency, the Assistant Program Coordinator is responsible for the day-to-day execution of these policies. This involves a great deal of administrative work, and coordination of the department's staff of program specialists.

The Assistant Program Coordinator is responsible for managing the flow of information within his or her department. This might mean setting up meetings with the staff, working with individual program specialists to monitor their budgets, allocating clerical and secretarial help to the particular individuals who need it, or creating and managing computer systems or other special office systems for the department.

The program coordinator may ask the Assistant Program Coordinator to undertake the nuts-and-bolts planning for a particular issue. For instance, if the program coordinator for art education feels that rural and inner-city school systems need more attention from the agency, the Assistant Program Coordinator would be dispatched to meet with school officials and with legislators; he or she would also read the literature on the issue and synthesize the attitudes of the program specialists into a report, which would then be evaluated department-wide and eventually be presented to the deputy director and executive director. The Assistant Program Coordinator is also intimately involved in the construction of the department's budget. He or she collects information from each specialist and assists the program coordinator in developing a proposal for the deputy director for budget and administration.

The level of responsibility of the Assistant Program Coordinator varies from agency to agency. In a large organization he or she may have significant planning responsibility, whereas in a smaller agency the job may be similar in status to that of an administrative aide.

In addition, the Assistant Program Coordinator may:

• personally run one or more programs within his or her area

• prepare and distribute memos about the department's activities to the rest of the agency staff

Salaries

Salaries range from $23,000 to $35,000.

Employment Prospects

This position can be an entry-level job for applicants with degrees in the arts or arts administration; in a larger agency, it could be quite competitive to get. It is often possible to rise to this position from the post of program specialist or assistant program specialist.

Advancement Prospects

If this job is mostly administrative, advancement prospects are only fair; but if one is able to undertake a good deal of management planning, then it is possible to advance to the position of program coordinator.

Education

An undergraduate degree in the field served by the agency department is necessary, and an advanced degree in this area or in arts administration is desirable.

Experience and Skills

Above all, the Assistant Program Coordinator must have exceptional organizational and administrative skills. The ability to undertake a complex research project, drawing from several types of sources, is also important. Knowledge of government agencies and the way they work is an advantage. The Assistant Program Coordinator must be able to work with many staff members and help to communicate their attitudes to his or her direct superiors and to the top management of the agency.

PROGRAM COORDINATOR

CAREER PROFILE

Duties: Manage cluster of related programs in the funding agency

Alternate Title: Director of an agency division

Salary Range: $25,000 to $60,000

Employment Prospects: Poor to fair

Advancement Prospects: Fair to good

Prerequisites:

Education—Undergraduate degree in the arts or related field

Experience—Background in arts administration, preferably in a government setting

Special Skills—Political acumen; ability to communicate, write well and respond to the arts community

CAREER LADDER

```
┌─────────────────────────────────────┐
│                                      │
│  Deputy Director for Programming     │
│                                      │
└─────────────────────────────────────┘

┌─────────────────────────────────────┐
│                                      │
│  Program Coordinator                 │
│                                      │
└─────────────────────────────────────┘

┌─────────────────────────────────────┐
│                                      │
│  Program Specialist                  │
│                                      │
└─────────────────────────────────────┘
```

Position Description

A Program Coordinator manages a cluster of related activities within the agency—for instance, programs relating to museum education or contemporary art. With the deputy director for programming or the deputy director for budget and administration, Program Coordinators lead planning, policy development and evaluation within the area they are responsible for.

The Program Coordinator manages a group of program specialists who are directly reponsible for a single granting category. For instance, the Program Coordinator managing grants for art education might supervise program specialists who offer grants to high schools, to museums or to artists who work with children directly. The Program Coordinator is responsible for developing and maintaining meaningful cooperation among these related program specialists. If the Program Coordinator learns of a special need in the field, he or she might make available a grant category composed of individual programs under his or her supervision.

The Program Coordinator develops budget plans within his or her area, allocates staff resources, monitors budget expenditures and makes decisions concerning shifts in emphasis within the area. For instance, the Program Coordinator for art education may decide to increase funding opportunities for inner-city and rural school systems which have the fewest art-related programs. Although any changes must be approved by a deputy director, Program Coordinators generate most planning proposals since they are more aware than anyone else of the changing needs in the areas they serve.

In addition, the Program Coordinator must serve as a spokesperson for the agency within a particular area. He or she must shape the tone and presentation of information about his or her programs and solicit comment and response from the field on the effectiveness of the agency's activities. All programs must be evaluated by the coordinator and his or her staff. Ultimately these studies are presented to the deputy and executive directors.

In addition the Program Coordinator may:

• run one or more specific programs personally
• attend professional meetings and conferences in his or her field
• publish articles on funding strategies for art-related publications

Salaries

Salaries for Program Coordinators range from $25,000 to $45,000, although they can be as high as $55,000 to $60,000.

Employment Prospects

The position of Program Coordinator is a dynamic job filled with the satisfaction of serving the arts. It is therefore a position quite difficult to get. Successful applicants should prove an extensive knowledge of a particular program area, experience in the field and excellent administrative abilities. Previous experience in government would improve one's chances.

Advancement Prospects

It is possible that the Program Coordinator can advance to the position of deputy director. However, it is unlikely that this promotion would take place before several years of distinguished service as a coordinator.

Education

An undergraduate degree in the appropriate program area—for instance, art education—and an advanced degree in that area or in administration are typically required.

Experience and Skills

The Program Coordinator must have excellent knowledge of the field he or she is working in and must know how to communicate with the constituency served through personal contacts, professional meetings and art publications. The Program Coordinator must be well versed in the methods of gathering information and proposing programs to address a particular need. He or she must be capable of managing a budget of as much as several million dollars. Since the Program Coordinator is the field representative for an area of the agency's activity, he or she must have excellent speaking and writing skills.

DEPUTY DIRECTOR FOR PROGRAMMING

CAREER PROFILE

Duties: Manage policymaking and personnel related to the funding programs of the agency

Salary Range: $35,000 to $50,000

Employment Prospects: Poor to fair

Advancement Prospects: Good to excellent

Prerequisites:

Education—Undergraduate degree in arts or art administration; graduate degree an advantage

Experience—Background in arts administration in a government or museum setting

Special Skills—Excellent policymaking skills and management capacity; ability to work with people; excellent writing and speaking skills

CAREER LADDER

```
┌─────────────────────────────┐
│                             │
│     Executive Director      │
│                             │
└─────────────────────────────┘

┌─────────────────────────────┐
│                             │
│     Program Coordinator     │
│                             │
└─────────────────────────────┘

┌─────────────────────────────┐
│                             │
│      Program Specialist     │
│                             │
└─────────────────────────────┘
```

Position Description

Since the executive director spends a good deal of his or her time out of the office, representing the funding agency, the day-to-day administration of the organization is left to the deputy directors. The Deputy Director for Programming is responsible for managing policymaking as well as the personnel related to the funding programs of the agency. He or she also supervises the dissemination of information about the agency's programs to the public as well as to relevant government officials.

One of the most important goals of an arts funding agency is to apply its allotted money to the most productive possible uses—whether directly to artists or to organizations which serve them. The Deputy Director for Programming undertakes an ongoing evaluation of need in the field, and devises appropriate responses on the part of the funding agency. For instance, in order to develop a new funding initiative—like a program to support the creation of new works by artists—the Deputy Director identifies the key issues and assesses the need for, and potential efficacy of, this program by assigning staff members to undertake research in the field. The Deputy Director then evaluates this research and makes recommendations to the executive director. If the recommendation is accepted the Deputy Director must assign or hire the required personnel to manage the new initiative.

The Deputy Director for Programming directly manages the program coordinators in each area of the agency's activity, as well as the public information government relations officer. He or she must monitor the procedures and programs in each of these areas and discuss future plans with these staff members. The Deputy Director must anticipate the need for human and financial resources in the areas he or she manages and articulate these needs to the executive director as well as the deputy director for budget and administration.

Although the executive director is the primary representative of the agency in the community, the Deputy Director for Programming must also occasionally play a role in the articulation of the goals and programs of the agency.

In addition the Deputy Director for Programming might:

* have considerable responsibility in creating the annual budget
* participate in the establishment of a personnel policy
* lobby government officials in particular program areas the agency serves

Salaries

Salaries vary from state to state and in federal agencies, but typically range from $35,000 to $50,000.

Employment Prospects

Competition is tough for this position. It is necessary for the applicant to have several years' experience in arts management and the proven ability to plan and articulate community needs in the arts.

Advancement Prospects

The chances are very good that a Deputy Director for Programming could advance to the position of executive director, either in the agency he or she works for, or in another similar organization. Prospects are better if the Deputy Director has demonstrated an excellent ability to lobby with the government and articulate the goals of the agency to the public and the arts community.

Education

An undergraduate degree in an area of the arts or the humanities, in addition to a graduate degree in a similar area, or management-related studies, is usually required.

Experience and Skills

The Deputy Director for Programming must have an outstanding ability to understand the needs of a community and create programs which serve those needs. This requires an excellent grasp of the steps required to plan new programs, as well as a sensitivity to artists and the arts. This job involves a great deal of personnel management, so the Deputy Director must be good with people and be able to understand and counsel them on their career goals. The Deputy Director must have an expert knowledge of at least one area of the arts, as well as excellent writing and speaking skills. He or she should also have experience dealing with the government, and have the capacity to lobby effectively.

PUBLIC INFORMATION OFFICER

CAREER PROFILE

Duties: Communicates goals and activities of agency to the general public and the government

Alternate Title: Director of Public Relations

Salary Range: $25,000 to $40,000

Employment Prospects: Fair

Advancement Prospects: Fair to good

Prerequisites:
Education—Undergraduate degree in journalism, public relations or political science

Experience—Extensive background in public relations and government; press connections or experience

Special Skills—Excellent writing and speaking skills; political acumen

CAREER LADDER

```
┌─────────────────────────────┐
│     Deputy Director for      │
│   Budget and Administration  │
└─────────────────────────────┘

┌─────────────────────────────┐
│                             │
│  Public Information Officer  │
│                             │
└─────────────────────────────┘

┌─────────────────────────────┐
│         Journalist/          │
│  Public Relations Professional │
└─────────────────────────────┘
```

Position Description

The Public Information Officer seeks to communicate the goals and activities of the funding agency, both to the general public, particularly through the press, and to the government bodies, like state legislatures, which oversee the funding agency. For this reason the Public Information Officer must have an excellent knowledge of politics and public relations, and also a total grasp of the kinds of grants the funding agency disperses.

In most cases the Public Information Officer produces the program guidelines for particular granting programs in concert with a program specialist. He or she must take copy from the program specialist, edit it for publication and coordinate the design and production of guidelines. The Public Information Officer must also prepare and distribute press releases on the activities of the funding agency, publish a newsletter in order to publicize particular programs and overall goals, and produce an annual report which summarizes the funding agency's accomplishments. All of these tools are used to increase awareness of the funding agency among the general public as well as among government officials.

Representatives of a funding agency are often asked to speak to community groups or special-interest arts organizations. The Public Information Officer lectures regularly, and may help coach other funding agency staff members in public speaking. The person in this position may also write important speeches for the executive director, especially when they are delivered to an audience of government officials.

The Public Information Officer may sometimes write articles about the funding agency to be published in an outside publication, or hold press conferences to make important policy announcements. He or she must stay in close touch with the funding agency's administrative and program staff in order to be aware of the ongoing goals and programs of the organization, and to receive their input into his public relations efforts.

In addition the Public Information Officer may:
- write special evaluation reports on funding agency programs
- maintain a photographic file of funding agency activities
- seek interviews in the press for the executive director or other funding agency staff

Salaries

The salary ranges between $25,000 and $35,000 but may be as high as $40,000.

Employment Prospects

This is a highly sensitive position requiring political savvy, strategic thinking and excellent writing skills. Competition is therefore quite brisk for the position and requires a good deal of previous experience in the areas of public relations or government.

Advancement Prospects

Advancement to the position of deputy director of planning is possible, but only likely if the Public Information Officer has become intimately involved with policy issues at the funding agency.

Education

An undergraduate degree in journalism, public relations, political science or the arts is necessary. Graduate work in any of these areas is an advantage.

Experience and Skills

Like all public relations professionals, the Public Information Officer should have a wide network of contacts in the press, excellent writing skills and superior public speaking ability. A background in journalism or television news would be a great advantage. In communicating with government officials, the Public Information Officer must have excellent interpersonal and negotiation skills. He or she must be aware of the processes of producing publications, and must have a great sensitivity to the arts and particularly the goals of the funding agency itself.

DEPUTY DIRECTOR FOR BUDGET AND ADMINISTRATION

CAREER PROFILE

Duties: Manage the personnel and financial policy issues in the agency

Salary Range: $30,000 to $55,000

Employment Prospects: Fair

Advancement Prospects: Fair

Prerequisites:

Education—Undergraduate or graduate degree in business administration or arts administration

Experience—Extensive background in financial and personnel management, preferably in a government setting

Special Skills—Ability to plan budgets; administer accounting and other financial systems; knowledge of personnel standards; ability to work well with people

CAREER LADDER

```
┌─────────────────────────────┐
│                             │
│     Executive Director      │
│                             │
└─────────────────────────────┘

┌─────────────────────────────┐
│    Deputy Director for      │
│  Budget and Administration  │
│                             │
└─────────────────────────────┘

┌─────────────────────────────┐
│                             │
│        Accountant           │
│                             │
└─────────────────────────────┘
```

Position Description

The Deputy Director for Budget and Administration manages the financial and personnel policy issues within the funding agency. He or she is supervised by the executive director, but works in tandem with the deputy director for programming to run the agency day-to-day. Since the major objective of an arts funding agency is the dispersal of money, the management of budgets and contracts with grant recipients is a central activity for someone in this position.

The Deputy Director for Budget and Administration constructs the agency's budget by collecting information from program and administrative staff, as well as from the legislators who fund the agency. He or she plans the sequence of budget negotiations with staff members and then monitors money spent. In most funding agencies recipients of grants are required to submit substantial documentation of how they spend public funds. This documentation must be reviewed by the deputy director for budget and administration. He or she must also be available to answer questions from grant applicants with regard to budgets and the timetable for receiving funds.

This position also includes the planning and implementation of personnel policies, including the

establishment of salary levels, undertaking staff evaluations, and designing benefit packages. Since funding agencies are part of the government, rigorous personnel standards typically apply to its employees. The Deputy Director must be aware of these policies and be sure they are implemented agency-wide. He or she is also responsible for the process of hiring new employees and planning staff training and orientation programs.

There are many administrative tasks that fall to the Deputy Director for Budget and Administration. He or she may regularly supervise the administrative staff of the agency, from secretaries to accountants. The responsibility for maintenance of the offices of a building may also fall on the shoulders of the Deputy Director. He or she may submit an annual financial report to the legislature, or be called into hearings or negotiations of a financial nature.

In addition the Deputy Director for Budget and Administration may:

- plan and implement a schedule of staff meetings for the entire agency

- manage the purchase and utilization of office equipment and other capital expenditures

Salaries

Salaries range from $30,000 to $55,000, but may be significantly higher in a national or large state agency.

Employment Prospects

Competition is fairly difficult for this position. An applicant needs solid experience—usually several years—in administration for nonprofit organizations, and significant experience managing personnel. The position might attract applicants from the private sector or non-art-related government agencies, as well as people interested in the arts.

Advancement Prospects

Unless the Deputy Director for Budget and Administration has an excellent ability to articulate the agency's goals publicly, it is unlikely that he or she will advance to the position of executive director. However, the administrative experience gained in this position is rigorous and impressive and might prepare the Deputy Director for a government job with more authority, or a position in a major museum as director of finance.

Education

This position requires a financial background with a sensitivity to the arts. Although an undergraduate degree in the humanities might be attractive, an advanced degree in business, personnel management or nonprofit administration is usually required.

Experience and Skills

The Deputy Director for Budget and Administration must have a thorough grasp of accounting, budgetmaking and the legal aspects of disbursing public funds. He or she must have some experience working with federal or state legislatures. An excellent grasp of personnel management procedures is necessary, as are the ability to work well with people and the capacity to settle disputes among employees and clarify agency policies. An enthusiasm for the agency's art-related mission is an advantage, as are public speaking and writing skills.

EXECUTIVE DIRECTOR

CAREER PROFILE

Duties: Direct programmatic and financial policy of the agency; represent its programs to the public and the government

Salary Range: $50,000 to $100,000

Employment Prospects: Poor

Advancement Prospects: Good

Prerequisites:

Education—Undergraduate degree in the arts or humanities; graduate degree in the humanities or business administration

Experience—Extensive background in arts administration, preferably in a government setting

Special Skills—Excellent policymaking skills; superior communications skills; political acumen

CAREER LADDER

```
┌─────────────────────────────┐
│                             │
│     Executive Director      │
│                             │
└─────────────────────────────┘

┌─────────────────────────────┐
│                             │
│       Deputy Director       │
│                             │
└─────────────────────────────┘

┌─────────────────────────────┐
│                             │
│     Program Coordinator     │
│                             │
└─────────────────────────────┘
```

Position Description

Public funding agencies, like federal endowments for the arts or state councils on the arts, are an important source of monies for most arts organizations. Although many have endowments which cover the expenses of building operation and other forms of overhead, public funds are often crucial for the execution of special projects or programs. The National Endowment for the Arts and the National Endowment for the Humanities, as well as most state arts councils, fund arts of all media from theater and music to every area of the visual arts, including individual artists. Since these funding agencies are government bodies, the Executive Director spends a good deal of time communicating with state or federal legislatures about the condition of the arts in the areas he or she serves. The Executive Director is the primary lobbyist for the arts and for the agency's funding allocation. The Executive Director must be able to maintain a high profile in the arts community: By speaking with its leaders, he or she is able to develop the kind of policies which will best serve the field.

The Executive Director is also the leader within the agency and must set programmatic goals as well as agency standards for dispensing funds to artists and arts organizations. By dispensing federal or state funds, these agencies enter into many types of contracts with those who receive money. The Executive Director works with his or her staff to structure these relationships to ensure that government funds have been spent as they should, and that the process of calling for, receiving and documenting the use of funds by the funded organizations is as smooth and expeditious as possible.

The Executive Director must also answer to the steering committee of the funding agency. Often, grant awards are not final until this advisory body approves each decision. The Director may also have some direct responsibility for managing personnel.

In addition, the Executive Director might:

- spearhead a special arts initiative in any of the areas the agency serves

- organize symposia on the arts or other major public information events

- make formal reports to government officials about the status of the arts in a particular community or area.

Salaries

Depending upon the pay scales of different cities, states, or the federal government, the Executive Director may make between $50,000 and $100,000.

Employment Prospects

The position of Executive Director of a funding agency is very competitive and difficult to obtain. The applicant must combine experience and expertise in political lobbying with a solid knowledge of a wide range of the arts and an excellent grasp of the role that they play in the community. Few people combine those qualities well. In some cases, especially in the federal government, this position is a political appointment.

Advancement Prospects

As the head of a funding agency, the Executive Director has nowhere to advance to within the organization. However, he or she may go on to direct another government agency in either the arts or a related area.

Education

The Executive Director should have an undergraduate degree in one area of the arts or in a related humanities field. An advanced degree in business or management or in the arts is also required.

Experience and Skills

Above all the Executive Director must be a skillful representative of the arts within government, and of government within the arts. This requires a great deal of tact, eloquence and political know-how. The Executive Director must be a person who knows how to get things done in the midst of bureaucracy. He or she must also be able to understand and articulate the various and sometimes contradictory goals of the arts community. The Executive Director must be able to evaluate areas of need and interest, and to use this information to lead an effective planning process.

SECTION 6
ART JOURNALISM

PRODUCTION ASSISTANT

CAREER PROFILE

Duties: Assist in technical production of magazine design

Salary Range: $10,000 to $20,000

Employment Prospects: Fair to good

Advancement Prospects: Poor to fair

Prerequisites:
   Education—Undergraduate degree in graphic design

   Experience—Background in technical design and pasteup

   Special Skills—Excellent organizational ability and attention to detail

CAREER LADDER

```
┌─────────────────────────────┐
│         Designer            │
└─────────────────────────────┘

┌─────────────────────────────┐
│     Production Assistant    │
└─────────────────────────────┘

┌─────────────────────────────┐
│    Graphic Design School    │
└─────────────────────────────┘
```

Position Description

The Production Assistant helps the designer with the technical aspects of putting together a magazine. The process of preparing the periodical for publication includes many steps, and in a magazine which comes out frequently, there is always great pressure to meet deadlines. When articles, columns, headlines and other text are received by the magazine they must be sent out to a typesetter to be executed in a specific type. Illustrations are received in standard sizes, and the percentages by which they need to be reduced or enlarged have to be calculated by the designer or the Production Assistant. Once these raw materials are received, the copy must be laid out on special boards from which the printer creates the final product.

The Production Assistant is responsible for organizing all of this material and then accomplishing the physical pasteup. This includes cutting long columns of typeset copy and fitting them into the page size of the periodical. The Production Assistant must therefore be extremely vigilant that he or she transposes copy accurately. In positioning photographs on the page and reducing or enlarging them, the Production Assistant must be aware of reversing images or incorrectly cropping them.

In the process of preparing the publication for printing, there is a great deal of shuttling back and forth between the printer and the magazine's offices. Depending upon the size of the operation and the volume of work given to the Production Assistant, he or she may be used to transport materials back and forth or to make other pickups and deliveries of design-related materials.

On a small magazine the Production Assistant may be hired on a part-time basis only, whereas on a major publication with a more complex graphic identity, he or she may be a very busy, full-time employee who grows to have significant input into certain aspects of the magazine's design.

In addition the Production Assistant may:
- coordinate design-related bills
- do research on graphic styles
- provide occasional secretarial support for the editorial staff

Salaries

The Production Assistant may make as little as $6 to $10 per hour on a part-time basis, or from $10,000 to $20,000 full-time.

Employment Prospects

Since the Production Assistant works primarily on the technical design of the publication and has relatively little input into a graphic concept, it is possible to enter this position with little more experience than a proficiency in pasteup skills. Magazines often work with a pool of free-lance Production Assistants.

Advancement Prospects

Unless the Production Assistant demonstrates excellent conceptual design skills in the process of his or her technical work, it is unlikely that he or she will advance to the position of designer. However, being a Production Assistant in a creatively designed publication can prepare one for further education, or a better job elsewhere.

Education

A degree in graphic design or other training in the technical processes of design is required. Coursework in art or art history is an advantage.

Experience and Skills

The Production Assistant must have expert skills in pasteup and the other technical processes of design. A knowledge of printing methods and practices is invaluable as is a sensitivity to art and art history. Since the Production Assistant must follow the instructions of the designer carefully, he or she must be an organized, hardworking person who is able to meet strict deadlines.

DESIGNER

Duties: Responsible for conceptual and technical design of the magazine

Salary Range: $12,000 to $40,000

Employment Prospects: Fair

Advancement Prospects: Fair to good

Prerequisites:

Education—Undergraduate or graduate degree in graphic design

Experience—Significant experience in conceptual and technical design

Special Skills—Sensitivity to art, and the ability to create a framework for the fine arts; superior conceptual design skills

CAREER LADDER

```
┌─────────────────────────────┐
│            Editor           │
└─────────────────────────────┘

┌─────────────────────────────┐
│           Designer          │
└─────────────────────────────┘

┌─────────────────────────────┐
│     Production Assistant     │
└─────────────────────────────┘
```

Position Description

An art magazine's design can be a fundamental expression of its editorial policy. Some magazines favor straightforward layouts, whereas others employ special graphic techniques which can convey specific messages about the magazine's point of view, such as a sense of contemporaneity or the desire to reach a broad public. Not only is the Designer responsible for preparing the magazine for publication, but with the editor he or she is involved with creating a design identity for the publication.

Some major magazines change their graphic design conventions annually or every few years, but usually maintain a consistent look throughout a single year. In order to develop a design concept, the Designer must be aware of other periodicals serving similar audiences as well as the types of articles that will be published in the magazine. With this background knowledge, he or she works closely with the editor, making proposals and mock-ups of alternative design concepts, one of which will ultimately win approval.

Within established design guidelines for a publication, there is always a significant amount of flexibility. Therefore, for every issue of the periodical the Designer must assess the material to be included and organize it visually. This includes choosing typeset styles, illustrations and special graphic elements, if desired or necessary. The Designer should stay true to the look of the magazine, but he or she may also come up with creative new solutions for presenting the changing content from issue to issue. One of the most important elements of any magazine is its cover, and the Designer must devote a good deal of time and energy to choosing illustrations and/or graphics which will make it eye-catching and individualistic.

In addition to his or her considerable work in creating design concepts with the editorial staff, the Designer has a large amount of technical pasteup work to do for every issue. Smaller art magazines may be quite low on support staff, so that the Designer must supervise the typesetting, the preparation of illustrations and the physical preparation of the boards from which the printer works. Usually the Designer coordinates negotiations with the printer, and he or she is always on hand during the actual printing to ensure that color illustrations are accurate and all other specifications are followed.

In addition the Designer may:
- engage a photographer to make special pictures for the publication
- design promotional materials for the periodical
- assist advertisers in designing their ads

Salaries

Depending upon the size of the magazine the Designer makes between $12,000 and $40,000.

Employment Prospects

Since art magazine editors are visually oriented, they are usually very particular about the person they choose to design their publication. Although salaries tend to be lower than in a corporate design setting, competition can be intense, and an extensive background in publishing, with a distinguished portfolio of art-related projects, is usually necessary for a major publication. In a smaller art magazine, chances are better that one may be employed with only moderate experience.

Advancement Prospects

Most art magazines have a single Designer, so there is little room to grow within the publication itself. However, association with a prestigious art magazine can prepare one for greater challenges in other organizations, whether they be art-related or not.

Education

The Designer should have a degree in graphic design, with training in both design conception and technical pasteup. Any additional art or art history-related training can be an advantage.

Experience and Skills

The Designer of an art magazine must have a great sensitivity to art and art history. There is a delicate balance between the photographs of works of art and the design into which they fit. The Designer must be able to strike a balance between his or her concept and the works of art published. Knowledge of art history and art criticism is invaluable in this position. The Designer must be able to establish a good rapport with the editor and the writers for the magazine. Excellent technical and conceptual design skills are necessary, as is considerable experience in producing periodicals.

CRITIC

CAREER PROFILE

Duties: Review exhibitions; write feature articles about art and artists

Salary Range: 0 to $40,000

Employment Prospects: Poor

Advancement Prospects: Fair

Prerequisites:

Education—Undergraduate or graduate degree in art history

Experience—Extensive background in writing about art

Special Skills—Superior writing ability; excellent knowledge of art and art history; ability to conceptualize critically

CAREER LADDER

```
┌─────────────────────────────┐
│                             │
│          Editor             │
│                             │
└─────────────────────────────┘

┌─────────────────────────────┐
│                             │
│     Contributing Editor     │
│                             │
└─────────────────────────────┘

┌─────────────────────────────┐
│                             │
│          Critic             │
│                             │
└─────────────────────────────┘
```

Position Description

Working as an art Critic is one of the most difficult positions in the arts. Not only is it hard to get your work into print, but even if you do, the pay is usually very low. Most critics start by writing reviews or short articles for small publications, either for a very small fee or for no money at all. Once a Critic has built up a significant body of writing, he or she can then approach major or intermediate publications. It may take several years before one can actually make a living from writing about art, and those who succeed at it are very few in number.

Art Critics write for newspapers, art magazines, general-interest magazines and museum publications. Many Critics supplement their writing activity with teaching, curatorial work or some other form of regular employment. The job varies depending upon what the Critic writes for. Although working for a metropolitan newspaper or general-interest magazine can be lucrative and prestigious, the work one can do in this context is limited by the necessity of writing for a general-interest audience. Most art magazines have a group of free-lance Critics whose reviews or feature articles they regularly publish. Although art magazines offer Critics the opportunity to delve more deeply into the ideas surrounding art, these publications may not be able to offer work as regular or profitable as that of a staff position on a newspaper or general-interest publication. Once an art Critic establishes a reputation through hard work, talent and persistence, he or she may be offered opportunities to lecture or contribute essays to museum catalogues. Most art Critics balance their activities between regular relationships with publications and one-time free-lance opportunities.

There are many attitudes about how one should discuss art, and most Critics have developed a point of view. Some Critics are very interested in describing what artwork looks like and how it makes one feel; others are more concerned with the ideas that artists use to conceive their work. Art Critics who are known for strong and reasoned positions usually have a greater success in the field of art publishing than those with a journalistic bent, who are more suited to working for newspapers or general-interest magazines.

In addition a Critic may:
* undertake book-length projects
* curate exhibitions on a free-lance basis
* edit anthologies of critical writing

Salaries

At the beginning of a Critic's career he or she may make nothing, or next to nothing. Feature articles may bring fees ranging from less than $100 to thousands of dollars. A staff writer for a major general-interest magazine can make $40,000 or more.

Employment Prospects

Without years of experience, an impressive record of publications and an expert knowledge of one or several areas of art, art history, or critical theory, it is highly unlikely that one can obtain a position as an art Critic. In journalistic settings, such as a metropolitan newspaper, or in a small, locally focused art magazine, it is easier to get a first break, but even in these areas excellent writing skills and expert knowledge are required.

Advancement Prospects

For an art Critic, advancement means writing more extensively and for better publications. Professional growth may occur very slowly for an art Critic, requiring years of writing for minor or local publications. The best way of advancing is to keep thinking, writing and learning about one's field.

Education

Education can vary greatly for art critics. Some have no formal training in the field of art history; they know what they do through independent research and read-ing. Others have participated in formal degree programs in art history, art or criticism. Some art Critics have been trained in journalism programs. Ultimately, what counts is the quality of the writing and the Critic's judgments.

Experience and Skills

In addition to excellent writing skills and the ability and desire to stay abreast of a field of art history or critical theory, the good art Critic must have a skill which is difficult to quantify—the ability to elucidate works of art in an interesting way. The art Critic should have as much experience working with or speaking to artists as is possible, and must have written a great deal, since this is often the best way of perfecting one's critical skills. To succeed as an art Critic one must be persistent and resourceful. No matter how small a publication, the chance to publish a piece of writing is an important opportunity for the beginning art Critic.

TRANSLATOR

CAREER PROFILE

Duties: Translate reviews and articles from a foreign language to English

Salary Range: $20 to $100 per hour, or fee may be paid by the word

Employment Prospects: Fair

Advancement Prospects: Fair

Prerequisites:

Education—Undergraduate or graduate degree in art history or languages

Experience—Extensive translation experience, preferably in the context of the arts

Special Skills—Superior knowledge of one or more foreign languages, and excellent technical skills in English; editorial and writing skills

CAREER LADDER

```
┌─────────────────────────────────┐
│                                 │
│            Editor               │
│                                 │
└─────────────────────────────────┘

┌─────────────────────────────────┐
│                                 │
│        Assistant Editor         │
│                                 │
└─────────────────────────────────┘

┌─────────────────────────────────┐
│                                 │
│          Translator             │
│                                 │
└─────────────────────────────────┘
```

Position Description

The art world has become more and more international, increasing the pressure on American art magazines to include significant coverage of work that is happening in Europe, as well as in South America and other parts of the world. Often, however, it is difficult or impossible to find an English-speaking critic who knows enough about the work in these areas to write about them authoritatively. For this reason most art magazines with even a minor international focus employ part-time Translators. Although it is unlikely that one could work as an art magazine Translator full-time, it is a viable way for a multilingual critic to supplement his or her income.

As in all types of translation, the Translator who works for an art magazine must have a good general knowledge of, and sensitivity to, the articles he or she is translating. Often, a critic who has a good knowledge of another culture and an expert grasp of its language fills this position. When an article or review needs translation an editor at the art magazine contacts the Translator, who reads it, makes a draft translation which is sent to the author for comments, and then delivers the finished copy to the magazine. Because deadlines are always tight in a periodical, the Translator will probably have to complete his or her job quickly and accurately.

Although any one art magazine may have only a small volume of translation to do per issue, the number of people with sufficient language skills and knowledge of the arts to perform this function well is extremely small, so a Translator may be able to establish a good reputation and receive work from several sources. Working on an art magazine as a Translator may lead to other projects, such as foreign art book translation.

In addition the Translator may:
- do editorial work for the magazine, especially with foreign authors
- write reviews in English for the magazine
- do special research in areas of foreign art for the magazine

Salaries

A Translator may make $20 to $100 per hour, or more, or may be paid by the word.

Employment Prospects

Although there are limited opportunities for the Translator at art magazines, someone who combines the rare skills of an excellent knowledge of art with expert knowledge of one or more languages has a good chance, if interested in getting work. As with all freelance positions, the Translator must make his or her qualifications and potential services known to the magazine's editor, and perhaps work on a trial project before being formally hired.

Advancement Prospects

It is possible that a Translator who is a skilled writer or experienced editor may advance to a critic's position or an editorial post in the magazine, after trust has been established through translation jobs.

Education

An undergraduate degree in the arts or languages is necessary, and a graduate degree in the study of a foreign language may also be required.

Experience and Skills

The Translator must have experience making translations, preferably in the area of the arts. He or she must have an excellent grasp of English and be aware of the kinds of art criticism or historical writing which the art magazine publishes. Editorial experience or a background as a critic are invaluable in this position.

CONTRIBUTING EDITOR

CAREER PROFILE

Duties: Write and suggest articles for the art magazine

Salary Range: $5,000 to $40,000

Employment Prospects: Poor

Advancement Prospects: Fair

Prerequisites:

Education—Undergraduate or graduate degree in art history

Experience—Extensive background in critical writing; editorial experience

Special Skills—Superior writing skills; excellent knowledge of art in the field of the magazine

CAREER LADDER

```
┌─────────────────────────────┐
│                             │
│           Editor            │
│                             │
└─────────────────────────────┘

┌─────────────────────────────┐
│                             │
│      Contributing Editor     │
│                             │
└─────────────────────────────┘

┌─────────────────────────────┐
│                             │
│           Critic            │
│                             │
└─────────────────────────────┘
```

Position Description

A Contributing Editor does not work at the art magazine on a daily basis, but is usually a free-lance writer or critic who regularly writes articles for the publication. Instead of waiting to be asked by an editor to write a particular piece, the Contributing Editor suggests his or her own topics for approval by the editor. The Contributing Editor may also suggest other writers or topics for coverage in the magazine, while not writing them personally, and in such cases may have primary editorial responsibility for working with the author.

Since most art magazines must operate on a limited budget, working with Contributing Editors is a good way to expand editorial capacity without paying full-time salaries. Contributing Editors are especially effective for magazines which wish to cover regions or countries far from their editorial offices. A large American art magazine, for example, may have one or more Contributing Editors working in Europe who will suggest stories or exhibitions for review. Smaller magazines whose editorial offices are in one city may have Contributing Editors in other cities. Such an editor not only writes but also often coordinates a small group of free-lance writers.

Contributing Editors may also attend regular editorial meetings with the magazine's full-time staff. This is an important function, for they bring a fresh, "outsider" point of view into the inner circle of the publication. Often, because they have fewer administrative responsibilities than other editors, Contributing Editors are able to stay more aware of new developments or artists who warrant coverage.

Contributing Editors are usually writers first and editors second, so, like art critics, they must assiduously attend art exhibitions, visit artists and stay current with reading in the field. In most cases a critic must attain a broad and impressive reputation before he or she is asked to contribute to an art publication in this way. For many critics, though, it is a good way to maintain some degree of security while having the freedom to take outside jobs.

In addition the Contributing Editor may:

- write a regular column or correspondence for the magazine
- hire and dispatch free-lance writers in other towns or countries
- meet regularly with the editor

Salaries

Depending upon the extent of the Contributing Editor's involvement in the magazine, he or she may make as little as $5,000 or as much as $40,000. In some cases, the Contributing Editor is paid directly for articles or reviews.

Employment Prospects

One is not generally offered a position as a Contributing Editor for a major art magazine unless one has established an impressive reputation and publication record as a critic. There are also logistical limitations in some cases: For instance, if a magazine needs a Contributing Editor to cover a certain country or region, only people who know that area well are considered. Competition is very brisk, and opportunities are limited.

Advancement Prospects

Chances are good for a Contributing Editor to advance to the position of staff editor. In many cases, however, this is not desirable, for it means that the time the Contributing Editor could devote to actual writing would be reduced. The prestige of being a Conbributing Editor at a major art publication can greatly enhance one's reputation as an art critic.

Education

There is no standard education requirement, though in most cases an undergraduate degree in art history is necessary, and a graduate degree desirable. More important than formal education are the Contributing Editor's writing skills and knowledge of the field.

Experience and Skills

The Contributing Editor must be an experienced art critic or writer who has written widely and well in the areas of the art magazine's interest. An impressive publication record is necessary, as are good connections among writers and artists in one's field. Editorial skills and experience are usually required, though in most cases the Contributing Editor is valued primarily for his or her writing skills and ability to recognize important artists or movements which warrant coverage.

ASSISTANT EDITOR

CAREER PROFILE

Duties: Assist editor in preparing copy and illustrations for the magazine

Salary Range: $10,000 to $30,000

Employment Prospects: Poor to fair

Advancement Prospects: Fair to good

Prerequisites:

Education—Undergraduate or graduate degree in art history

Experience—Background in writing about art; some editorial skills

Special Skills—Excellent writing ability; knowledge of art and art history; good organizational and clerical talents

CAREER LADDER

```
┌─────────────────────────────────┐
│                                 │
│      Editor/Managing Editor      │
│                                 │
└─────────────────────────────────┘

┌─────────────────────────────────┐
│                                 │
│        Assistant Editor          │
│                                 │
└─────────────────────────────────┘

┌─────────────────────────────────┐
│      Editorial Assistant or     │
│            College or            │
│         Graduate School          │
└─────────────────────────────────┘
```

Position Description

There are hundreds of details associated with publishing a magazine, and small mistakes can translate into embarrassment for the publication. Working in tandem with the editor or managing editor, the Assistant Editor helps to bring the publication through the manuscript phase to a finished periodical. The specific duties of the Assistant Editor may vary greatly depending upon the size of the magazine and its staff organization. However, most art magazine staffs are small enough so that he or she may become involved in every aspect of editorial activity.

The Assistant Editor may spend a great deal of time proofreading manuscripts. Usually any piece of writing needs to be checked several times: before going to the typesetter, afterwards and then once more after the author has looked over the typeset copy. He or she may also assist in checking the accuracy of the author's factual assertions, or be asked to research the availability of photographs for the issue.

The Assistant Editor may be asked to read and respond to reader mail and to read unsolicited manuscripts in order to weed out promising articles from those the magazine is not interested in. He or she may also be asked to read and sort out press releases from galleries, museums and artists in order to assist the editor or managing editor in making decisions about what exhibitions to review.

Most art magazines are low on secretarial support. The Assistant Editor may provide typing, filing and other clerical assistance for the senior editorial staff. He or she may also be responsible for coordinating headlines or photo captions. The Assistant Editor may undertake research projects on art-historical or critical issues and maintain a library of source books or an archive of the magazine's back issues. Magazines are often flooded with miscellaneous requests from readers. An Assistant Editor may answer this correspondence and handle other types of mail in the office.

Like all members of an editorial staff, the Assistant Editor is often a jack-of-all-trades who may be writing a review of a gallery exhibition one day and typing the manuscript of another author the next.

In addition an Assistant Editor may:

- receive and route bills such as requests for writers' fees
- communicate with regular columnists or reviewers
- organize editorial meetings

Salaries

Depending upon the size of the art magazine, an Assistant Editor may make between $10,000 and $30,000.

Employment Prospects

Since the Assistant Editor is a junior member of the editorial staff, it can be an entry-level position. However, even with relatively little experience required, competition for this position can be intense. A distinguished educational record, or a background in writing about art, is usually necessary.

Advancement Prospects

The prospects for promotion are fair to good for an Assistant Editor. If he or she has been able to work directly with authors and to write a good deal on his or her own, or has become involved with forging an editorial policy for the magazine through working closely with the editor, chances are better for advancement. However, to rise to the position of editor at a major art magazine, one must have built a considerable reputation in the field.

Education

An undergraduate degree in art history or journalism may be sufficient for an Assistant Editor, though an advanced degree may be an advantage.

Experience and Skills

The Assistant Editor must have an excellent technical grasp of English and be proficient at proofreading. He or she should have a great sensitivity to art, art history and critical issues, and a lively curiosity about the field. Experience as a writer about art is invaluable, as are excellent research skills. The Assistant Editor must also be an expert typist, and preferably have experience in word processing. It is also an advantage in this position to have experience in producing a publication.

MANAGING EDITOR

CAREER PROFILE

Duties: Manage day-to-day editorial activity of the magazine

Salary Range: $12,000 to $50,000

Employment Prospects: Poor

Advancement Prospects: Good to excellent

Prerequisites:

Education—An undergraduate or graduate degree in art history, English or journalism

Experience—Extensive editorial experience, preferably on an art magazine

Special Skills—Excellent knowledge of magazines; superior grasp of English; good knowledge of art history; management skills

CAREER LADDER

```
+-------------------------+
|         Editor          |
+-------------------------+

+-------------------------+
|     Managing Editor     |
+-------------------------+

+-------------------------+
|     Assistant Editor    |
+-------------------------+
```

Position Description

In association with the editor, the Managing Editor is responsible for the day-to-day editorial activity of the magazine. Although the Managing Editor is typically consulted on editorial policies, he or she is primarily responsible for the nuts-and-bolts activities of bringing articles in and getting the publication ready to go to press. Most editorial staffs work collaboratively, so the editor and Managing Editor may share responsibilities almost equally on some periodicals.

The Managing Editor usually has responsibility for ongoing activities at the magazine. For instance, he or she may be charged with determining what exhibitions to review each issue, and what artists to ask to review them. This involves sifting through vast amounts of information in the form of press releases or photographs in order to decide what shows are significant and warrant coverage.

The Managing Editor may also supervise the processing of articles once they are received from writers. Like the editor, he or she may give suggestions with regard to grammar and content to the author and would also be responsible for sending copy to the typesetter, making sure it is properly proofread, reviewed with the writer and then dispatched to the designer. The Managing Editor may also work directly with the designer to ensure that he or she has

manuscripts and photographs when necessary, and that the magazine is proceeding through production on schedule.

In a large magazine where several editors are commissioning articles and working with writers, the Managing Editor must coordinate this activity, making sure that a particular issue has all of its articles, reviews or illustrations in order. In this context, he or she may also be responsible for the orderly management of office systems, including policies on answering correspondence from readers, or on reading and replying to unsolicited manuscripts.

The Managing Editor may supervise the magazine's editorial budget. He must work with the editorial staff to assess costs, plan a workable budget and then supervise expenditures throughout the year. His or her financially related activity may also include working closely with advertisers. Art magazines are a primary means for art galleries and museums to get the word out about their exhibitions. Often these ads require special design or other individual treatment which may fall into the province of the Managing Editor.

Although the specific duties of a Managing Editor may vary depending upon the structure of the publication, he or she is the person who makes sure that the complex process of publishing a magazine proceeds efficiently and smoothly.

In addition the Managing Editor may:
- write articles for the magazine
- write grants

Salaries

Depending on the size of the magazine, the Managing Editor may make between $12,000 and $50,000.

Employment Prospects

All art magazine editorial positions are difficult to get. Depending upon the structure of the publcation, the Managing Editor may have less to do with artistic direction than with the editorial and financial management of the magazine. In that case, magazine experience may be more important than an intimate knowledge of art. When the Managing Editor is deeply involved in editorial policy, he or she must have achieved an impressive publications and editorial record.

Advancement Prospects

In most art magazines, the editorial staff remains quite stable. Advancement may be difficult, but it also may be irrelevant in a major publication where the Managing Editor grows to have an important editorial voice. Only if the person in this position has been deeply involved in editorial policy is he or she likely to advance to the position of editor.

Education

The Managing Editor should have a degree in art history, journalism or English. Depending upon the level of scholarly content in the publication, he or she may need an advanced degree in art history.

Experience and Skills

The Managing Editor must have extensive experience in producing a periodical publication. He or she must be aware of the steps necessary for processing a manuscript, designing a publication and printing it. In addition, this person must be able to manage people as well as budgets. An excellent knowledge of art is a great asset, if not absolutely necessary. The ability to make decisions about editorial direction and artistic quality is also an important skill. Even more than the editor, the Managing Editor must be an excellent administrator who is thorough, careful and able to work under pressure.

EDITOR

CAREER PROFILE

Duties: Design and execute magazine's editorial policy

Alternate Title: Executive Editor

Salary Range: $15,000 to $50,000

Employment Prospects: Poor

Advancement Prospects: Fair to good

Prerequisites:

Education—Undergraduate or graduate degree in art history

Experience—Extensive editorial or writing background in the area of art covered by the magazine

Special Skills—Superior editorial and writing ability; the talent of accurately observing and predicting the art world's trends; good rapport with writers and artists

CAREER LADDER

```
+-------------------------------------+
|                                     |
|              Editor                 |
|                                     |
+-------------------------------------+

+-------------------------------------+
|                                     |
|          Managing Editor            |
|                                     |
+-------------------------------------+

+-------------------------------------+
|                                     |
|          Assistant Editor           |
|                                     |
+-------------------------------------+
```

Position Description

Art magazines are one of the primary means of communication among artists, museums, galleries and the other institutions of the art world. They range from inexpensive tabloids primarily focused on a regional community to vividly colored international journals which combine ideas from several nations. No matter what the scale of the magazine, its Editor is responsible for providing the publication with an appropriate focus on art-historical or critical issues.

The Editor must determine the magazine's overall policy, which includes deciding what critical or art-historical issues it will consistently cover, and what attitudes it will espouse openly, if any. The Editor is responsible for commissioning specific articles from appropriate writers. This means that the art magazine Editor must have an intimate knowledge of the community his or her publication serves; this expertise is gained by visiting exhibitions and artists and through talking to art critics about the issues which interest them. Some art magazines are very close to being academic journals, and their activity is closely associated with a particular group of writers or artists. Other magazines provide ''news'' about the art scene. Most combine some of both.

Once the Editor commissions an article from a writer, he or she continues to work with that person, first during the phase of conception and research and finally when the manuscript is submitted to the magazine. After reviewing the writer's draft, the Editor suggests grammatical or content changes for the author to consider. In a small magazine or tabloid the Editor may work with every writer directly, whereas in a larger magazine he or she may work with only a few authors, or only make final editorial decisions. In either case, the Editor has ultimate responsibility for the content of the publication.

In addition to working with writers, the Editor guides the designer in establishing the look of the periodical. Especially in an art magazine, the design concept can say a lot about editorial policies and beliefs: Finding the right design language is an important editorial issue. As the artistic chief of the magazine, the Editor must represent his or her publication in the community, and may be involved in soliciting advertising revenues or grants if the publication is organized as a nonprofit venture.

In addition the Editor may:

- manage all personnel issues at the publication
- commission special works by artists for the magazine
- write articles for the publication personally

Salaries

Depending upon the size of the publication, the Editor may make between $15,000 and $50,000.

Employment Prospects

There are very few art magazines, and consequently editorial positions are scarce—but highly desired for their excitement, prestige and the opportunity to affect what the world thinks about a particular artist or art movement. Competition is extremely brisk, and it is unlikely that one can enter a responsible editorial position without considerable experience in writing about art or organizing exhibitions. As with museum work, a good reputation and publications record is essential.

Advancement Prospects

The Editor is the top artistic post in a magazine. In a major publication, the Editor may stay in the position for several years, finally advancing to another job in publishing or in an arts organization. For an Editor of a smaller publication, chances are fair for advancement, though it is unlikely that someone managing a locally-directed publication would advance to one with national scope.

Education

An undergraduate degree in art history or a related field is necessary. For a publication with a strongly theoretical or art-historical focus an advanced degree is necessary. A degree in journalism may be sufficient for some art magazine jobs.

Experience and Skills

A good Editor must combine an intelligent, well-thought-out point of view with a rigorous knowledge of language and excellent writing skills. The Editor must be able to assess how the practice of art or art history is developing, through close observation and extensive reading of the important writing which is happening in his or her field. He or she must be able to establish good working relationships with artists and writers. A developed visual sensitivity, excellent interpersonal skills and the ability to work under a great deal of pressure are all necessary. An extensive background in critical or art-historical writing is invaluable.

SECTION 7
AUCTION GALLERIES

INFORMATION COORDINATOR

CAREER PROFILE

Duties: Respond to journalists' inquiries; assist with special events; handle Telexes; arrange tours

Alternate Title: Assistant Publicist

Salary Range: $12,000 to $15,000

Employment Prospects: Fair

Advancement Prospects: Fair

Prerequisites:

Education—Bachelor's degree required; background in art and/or public relations helpful

Experience—None

Special Skills—Writing ability; typing

CAREER LADDER

```
┌─────────────────────────────────┐
│           Publicist             │
└─────────────────────────────────┘

┌─────────────────────────────────┐
│     Information Coordinator      │
└─────────────────────────────────┘

┌─────────────────────────────────┐
│      Student or Secretary        │
└─────────────────────────────────┘
```

Position Description

The Information Coordinator assists the publicist in the day-to-day operations of the public relations department and assists with any special events undertaken to publicize the auction gallery. Ordinary duties include answering any questions for journalists writing about the gallery; handling Telexes and other special communications; arranging tours upon request; and helping to prepare press releases.

The special events responsibilities of the Information Coordinator may include helping to arrange teas or cocktail parties for people who can publicize the auction house. Such events are likely to fall outside the usual nine-to-five working hours.

Salaries

The Information Coordinator can expect a salary of between $12,000 and $15,000 per year.

Employment Prospects

There is a fair chance of finding a position as an Information Coordinator. There are not many such jobs, but the turnover is fairly rapid as people move on to other jobs inside or outside of the auction house.

Advancement Prospects

The Information Coordinator has a reasonable chance of moving up within the auction gallery. He or she could be promoted to the position of publicist or could move to a different administrative or expert department.

Education

A bachelor's degree is required for this job, preferably with some background in art and/or public relations.

Experience and Skills

No particular experience is necessary for this position, but any writing experience will be useful. The clerical duties of the Information Coordinator make good typing skills a must. In addition, excellent communications and writing skills are important.

Tips for Entry

Personal contacts are extremely helpful in obtaining a job as an Information Coordinator. Working as an intern or a secretary in an auction house can provide the opportunity to make such contacts.

PUBLICIST

CAREER PROFILE

Duties: Write and distribute press releases; liaison with expert departments; handle press relations; plan special events

Alternate Title: Public Relations Director

Salary Range: $16,000 to $20,000

Employment Prospects: Fair

Advancement Prospects: Poor

Prerequisites:

Education—Bachelor's degree; art and public relations background preferred

Experience—Previous work as an information coordinator or elsewhere in public relations

Special Skills—Writing ability, communications skills

CAREER LADDER

```
┌─────────────────────────────────┐
│                                 │
│           Publicist             │
│                                 │
└─────────────────────────────────┘

┌─────────────────────────────────┐
│                                 │
│      Information Coordinator     │
│                                 │
└─────────────────────────────────┘
```

Position Description

The Publicist at an auction gallery is responsible for publicizing the gallery and its auctions. The Publicist stays closely in touch with the various expert departments and prepares publicity for upcoming sales. This may involve press releases on important works that will be on sale or on the famous collectors who are selling the works, or on the prices expected for artwork at a certain auction.

The Publicist normally supervises a staff of information coordinators or assistants who handle routine press inquiries and perform the day-to-day functions of the department.

The Publicist must also have good contacts in the press in order to get the auction house's press releases run in newspapers and magazines. This publicity attracts customers to the auction gallery. Special events such as teas, cocktail parties and exhibition openings are also designed to bring the potential buyers into the auction house and make them aware of the works for sale.

Auctions may be geared to different suggested price ranges, so the Publicist has to target the right audience for the auction gallery's publicity. Information on an auction of major Impressionist paintings must be placed in upscale publications; details on a print auction will likely be targeted to a wider readership.

Salaries

A Publicist will be paid approximately $16,000 to $20,000 per year.

Employment Prospects

A qualified candidate has a fair chance of obtaining a Publicist position at an auction gallery. There are few such jobs, but the turnover is relatively great, making openings available.

Advancement Prospects

It is difficult to advance from the position of Publicist. Many Publicists leave the auction gallery business to seek employment as Publicists for art galleries or in public relations firms.

Education

The Publicist must have a bachelor's degree, preferably with some background in art or art history and in public relations.

Experience and Skills

Previous work in public relations—either within the auction gallery field or outside it—is essential.

Writing is the most important skill for a Publicist. In addition, the Publicist should have strong interpersonal skills in order to deal effectively with members of the press and with department managers within the auction gallery.

CUSTOMER SERVICE ASSISTANT

CAREER PROFILE

Duties: Answer customer questions, take phone bids, assist clients

Alternate Title: Administrative Assistant

Salary Range: $12,000 to $15,000

Employment Prospects: Fair

Advancement Prospects: Fair

Prerequisites:

Education—Bachelor's degree; some art background necessary

Experience—None

Special Skills—Communications skills, tact, typing

CAREER LADDER

```
┌─────────────────────────────┐
│  Customer Service Manager   │
└─────────────────────────────┘

┌─────────────────────────────┐
│  Customer Service Assistant │
└─────────────────────────────┘

┌─────────────────────────────┐
│    Student or Secretary     │
└─────────────────────────────┘
```

Position Description

The Customer Service Assistant is a jack-of-all-trades who works to help customers of the auction house. This entails answering customer service queries, taking sealed and telephone bids, assisting with details of credit or shipping, and so on.

It is important for the Customer Service Assistant to get to know the auction house's regular clientele. Serious buyers expect special service, and the Customer Service Assistant is responsible for providing extra help to important clients.

The Customer Service Assistant performs various clerical duties as directed by the department manager, and spends considerable time on the telephone in performing his or her duties. Evening work may be required, as many major auctions are held at night.

This is a good entry-level position for persons interested in the auction gallery business.

Salaries

Customer Service Assistants generally make between $12,000 and $15,000 per year.

Employment Prospects

Chances for a job as a Customer Service Assistant are fair. The number of such positions is limited, but the turnover is relatively rapid.

Advancement Prospects

Opportunities for advancement are also fair. The Customer Service Assistant can move up within the administrative sphere of the auction house or laterally into one of the expert departments.

Education

The Customer Service Assistant must have a bachelor's degree, with a least some background in art. An art or art history major may be preferred, but not required.

Experience and Skills

There are no particular experience requirements for this position, but any work with the public will be useful. A person who has served an internship in an auction gallery will have an advantage in obtaining a job as a Customer Service Assistant.

The clerical duties of the job make it necessary for the Customer Service Assistant to have good typing skills. In addition, the Customer Service Assistant should have excellent communications skills and the ability to deal helpfully and courteously with the public.

CUSTOMER SERVICE MANAGER

CAREER PROFILE

Duties: Manage customer service department; prepare seating plans for major auctions; know clientele; take bids; provide information to customers

Alternate Title: None

Salary Range: $16,000 to $20,000

Employment Prospects: Fair

Advancement Prospects: Fair

Prerequisites:

Education—Bachelor's degree; art background required

Experience—Previous work in an administrative department at an auction gallery

Special Skills—Communications skills; tact; typing

CAREER LADDER

Customer Service Manager

Customer Service Assistant

Position Description

The Customer Service Manager has an important position within the administration of the auction gallery. The customer service department is responsible for customer relations, for keeping both the regular clientele and the occasional buyer happy. The Customer Service Manager supervises a staff that takes care of the routine duties of the department, such as taking bids, giving information, answering questions, and so on.

The Customer Service Manager also has responsibility for becoming familiar with the regular clientele of the gallery and being sensitive to their needs. The Manager must be able to discern which buyers are serious and which are not, and must be able to handle the politics of seating customers at important auctions. The actions of the Customer Service Manager can have a great influence on attracting and retaining regular clientele for the gallery by making each customer feel well taken care of.

Salaries

Customer Service Managers can expect to make a salary of between $16,000 and $20,000 per year.

Employment Prospects

There is a fair chance of a qualified individual's being able to find a position as a Customer Service Manager. Such positions are not numerous, but the turnover is fairly steady.

Advancement Prospects

The Customer Service Manager has a fair opportunity to advance to another position within the auction house, particularly if he or she is interested in making a lateral move to another administrative department or to an expert department.

Education

The Customer Service Manager must have a bachelor's degree and should have either a major or a minor in art or art history.

Experience and Skills

It is necessary for the aspiring Customer Service Manager to have had previous experience as an assistant in the customer service department of an auction gallery, or in a related department, such as advertising or public relations.

The Customer Service Manager must have excellent communications skills and should work well with the public. It is important to be tactful and to have strong social skills. Because of the clerical duties of the position, it is also necessary to have good typing ability.

DEPARTMENT ASSISTANT

CAREER PROFILE

Duties: Perform appraisals; locate artwork for sale; research artwork; assist in arranging sales

Alternate Title: None

Salary Range: $13,000 to $15,000

Employment Prospects: Fair

Advancement Prospects: Fair

Prerequisites:

Education—Bachelor's degree; art background preferred

Experience—None

Special Skills—Communications skills; ability to work well with people

CAREER LADDER

```
┌─────────────────────────────┐
│                             │
│     Department Manager      │
│                             │
└─────────────────────────────┘

┌─────────────────────────────┐
│                             │
│    Department Assistant     │
│                             │
└─────────────────────────────┘

┌─────────────────────────────┐
│                             │
│    Student or Secretary     │
│                             │
└─────────────────────────────┘
```

Position Description

A Department Assistant works in an expert department (e.g., contemporary art, American paintings, or prints) acquiring items for sale, arranging auctions, appraising pieces, preparing catalogues and working with important customers.

The position of Department Assistant is really a training job. The assistant works closely with the department manager, learning how to find and appraise a specialized type of artwork and how to locate and cultivate potential buyers for that kind of work. This involves interaction with art dealers and collectors as well as estates and trusts.

The position may require some travel and will most likely entail night work, as many important auctions are held in the evening.

Salaries

Salaries for Department Assistants are generally in the $13,000 to $15,000 range.

Employment Prospects

Aspiring Department Assistants have a fair chance of landing such a job. There are usually many applicants for the assistant position, but the turnover tends to be rapid, making openings available.

Advancement Prospects

Advancement opportunities are fair for a Department Assistant. Chances for promotion are particularly good when the business climate is good and, conversely, poor when there is a turndown in the economy. A Department Assistant may be promoted to department manager or move into an administrative department within the auction house. Work as a Department Assistant can also be good experience for someone who wishes to work at an art gallery.

Education

The Department Assistant should have a bachelor's degree, with some background in art or art history.

Experience and Skills

There is no particular experience required of a Department Assistant.

Good communications skills are important in this position, and it is important for the jobholder to be able to deal comfortably with collectors and art dealers. Sales skills can be helpful, and a good eye for art is most valuable.

Tips for Entry

Some of the larger auction galleries offer courses in art; these can be a good background, and they present an opportunity to make contacts within the auction house. A few auction galleries offer internships, which can also get your foot in the door. Finally, an individual may be able to find a secretarial position at an auction house and work his or her way up from there.

DEPARTMENT MANAGER

CAREER PROFILE

Duties: Supervise expert department; find artwork to sell; perform appraisals; research important pieces; arrange sales; cultivate clientele

Alternate Titles: Vice-president; Department Head

Salary Range: $16,000 to $25,000

Employment Prospects: Fair

Advancement Prospects: Poor

Prerequisites:

Education—Bachelor's degree required; art background helpful

Experience—Work as an assistant in an expert or administrative department

Special Skills—Expert knowledge appropriate to the department; ability to deal with the public

CAREER LADDER

```
┌─────────────────────────────┐
│                             │
│   Department Manager        │
│                             │
└─────────────────────────────┘

┌─────────────────────────────┐
│                             │
│   Department Assistant      │
│                             │
└─────────────────────────────┘
```

Position Description

A Department Manager runs an expert department at an auction gallery. Examples of expert departments are American paintings, contemporary art, Oriental art, Impressionist paintings, Old Master paintings, prints, sculpture, and so on. The Department Manager is an expert at locating artwork for his or her department to sell and at appraising such artwork. This expertise is usually gained on the job while working as an assistant in the department.

The Manager generally is responsible for preparing several sales each year. This involves acquiring items to sell by researching, talking to collectors and traveling to see particular works; supervising the logistics of the sale; helping to prepare catalogues, advertising and press releases; appraising items for sale; and nurturing contacts with important collectors and dealers.

Many Department Managers, though not all, are licensed auctioneers. The licensing procedure, usually administered by the state involved, entails the submission of affidavits of good character, but does not usually require any particular educational background.

The Department Manager can make the department successful by carefully cultivating the important buyers in his or her field of expertise. Hence, social skills, communications skills, and sales ability are important.

Salaries

The Department Manager can expect to make a salary of between $16,000 and $25,000 per year, with even higher salaries available to those with more experience or special expertise.

Employment Prospects

A qualified applicant for the position of Department Manager has a fair chance of winning the job. There are few such positions, but the turnover in them is relatively rapid, making openings available.

Advancement Prospects

The opportunities for the Department Manager to advance are limited. Only a handful of senior positions exist in auction galleries. Some Department Managers may, however, move on to open their own auction houses or to work in the art gallery business.

Education

The prospective Department Manager must have a bachelor's degree with some background in art and art history.

Experience and Skills

On-the-job training is the most important preparation an individual can have for this post. Most of the knowledge one needs in order to appraise artwork is acquired while he or she works as an assistant in an expert department.

The Department Manager must have strong communications skills in order to assist with publicity, advertising and catalogue preparation. It is also critical for him or her to have developed an eye for good artwork and for what will sell, and to be able to deal easily with important customers.

Organizations and Associations

There are no organizations specifically for auction gallery employees. The National Auctioneers Association (see Appendix IV) might be useful to Department Managers who are also auctioneers.

SECTION 8
ART-RELATED BUSINESSES

PRINT PUBLISHER

Duties: Confer with artist, choose print medium, select publisher, sell prints

Alternate Title: Print Edition Producer

Salary Range: $10,000 to $60,000

Employment Prospects: Poor

Advancement Prospects: Poor

Prerequisites:

Education—Most have college degree, though no degree is required

Experience—Work in fine art book publishing or art gallery

Special Skills—Business ability, artistic taste, familiarity with techniques of printmaking

```
┌─────────────────────────────┐
│                             │
│      Print Publisher        │
│                             │
└─────────────────────────────┘

┌─────────────────────────────┐
│     Gallery Position        │
│            or               │
│    Publishing Position      │
└─────────────────────────────┘
```

Position Description

A Print Publisher produces prints—for example, lithographs, serigraphs or etchings—of an artist's work. The Publisher generally compiles a portfolio of the prints of the various artists with whom he or she works, then sells the portfolio to galleries and collectors.

The Publisher usually selects an artist with whom he or she would like to work on the basis of the artist's work and the Publisher's sense of whether prints of such work will sell. Depending on the way the Publisher prefers to work, the actual ideas regarding the project can come from the artist or from the Publisher. It may take weeks or months to develop an artistic concept for a print series.

Once the artwork is completed, the Publisher works as the liaison with the printer who will be making the prints. It is not necessary for the Publisher to have printmaking skills, but it is important that he or she is well versed in the printmaking process, so that he or she can evaluate different printers and assure high-quality work.

The completed prints are owned by the Publisher, who retains financial responsibility throughout the entire process. The Publisher makes arrangements to pay the artist and the printer according to an agreed-upon formula. It is then the function of the Print Publisher to market the prints to galleries and collectors. This can be done in person, through a sales force or through catalogues. When selling prints personally, the Publisher will find that it is important to have extensive contacts in the art world, so that he or she can locate and target potential customers.

This is essentially an entrepreneurial job, for a person with previous experience as an art dealer, a fine art book publisher or a gallery salesperson.

Salaries

It is difficult to determine what initial compensation would be for a Print Publisher, but a moderately successful person just starting out might expect to earn from $10,000 to $30,000 a year. As the business grows, profits might increase to $60,000 per year or more.

Employment Prospects

It is fairly difficult to get started as a Print Publisher, as this is generally a self-employed position requiring start-up capital. Few Print Publishers employ assistants.

Advancement Prospects

As this is an entrepreneurial job, most Print Publishers regard it as a lifetime goal and do not expect to advance beyond it. Increased income and profitability might be regarded as a form of advancement.

Education

Though there are no formal educational requirements, most people in this work have college degrees.

Experience and Skills

It is essential that a Print Publisher have worked in an art gallery, in fine art book publishing, or as an art dealer in order to have the basic tools necessary to succeed.

The Publisher should be familiar with the printmaking process, though he or she need not actually have printmaking skills. In addition, a thorough understanding of business administration is very important.

Tips for Entry

The more experience and contacts one has in the art world, the better. In addition, a few large Print Publishers do hire assistants; working in this capacity could be very helpful in learning the business.

CORPORATE CURATOR

Duties: Acquire and place artwork for corporate collection; recordkeeping

Alternate Titles: None

Salary Range: $16,000 to $30,000

Employment Prospects: Good

Advancement Prospects: Fair

Prerequisites:

Education—Bachelor's degree in art or art history; master's degree preferred

Experience—Gallery or museum work

Special Skills—Artistic taste; understanding of corporate climate; ability to deal with all kinds of people

```
┌─────────────────────────┐
│                         │
│  Corporate Art Director │
│                         │
└─────────────────────────┘

┌─────────────────────────┐
│                         │
│   Corporate Curator     │
│                         │
└─────────────────────────┘

┌─────────────────────────┐
│                         │
│       Registrar         │
│                         │
└─────────────────────────┘
```

Position Description

A Corporate Curator works within a corporation's art program. Such programs generally are started when the corporation moves into a new building; important individuals within the firm see a need for an organized way to decorate the new surroundings while enriching the environment for employees and supporting the art community. Thus a formal program is begun to acquire artwork, place it in appropriate settings within the physical environment and undertake the necessary recordkeeping to keep track of the growing collection.

The Corporate Curator is involved with the purchase of artwork based on guidelines set down by the corporation. Many corporations form advisory boards of art professionals to guide them in their art acquisitions. The Curator is responsible for working within the given budget and for registrar-type tracking of the pieces within the collection, so a strong detail orientation and administrative skills are important.

This position is a unique one in the art world, in that the employees of the corporation who come into contact with the artwork may not be receptive to it. Some corporations purchase artwork that might be considered challenging to the workers—that is, not just a kind of pretty wallpaper—and the Corporate Curator must be sensitive to this. Therefore, the Curator should have strong communications skills and the ability to

deal with all kinds of people, such as artists, corporate executives, clerical workers.

Salaries

Entry-level salaries for Corporate Curators range from about $16,000 to $20,000, and can go higher for those with strong registrar experience. As one progresses within the field, salaries continue to range upward to about $30,000 per year.

Employment Prospects

Because this is an expanding area, with more companies starting formal art programs each year, employment prospects are good and continually growing.

Advancement Prospects

Advancement prospects for Corporate Curators are fair. There are usually two or more Curators working for an art program director, so upward movement is somewhat limited, but experience in this position is also good preparation for careers in gallery or museum work.

Education

A bachelor's degree in art or art history is essential, and a master's degree in art history, fine arts or arts administration is strongly preferred.

Experience and Skills

Any kind of art experience is helpful to those wishing to enter ths field. Experience requirements tend to be less formal and rigorous for Corporate Curators than for their museum counterparts. Recordkeeping and registrar experience, though, is especially valued in the corporate setting.

Though artistic taste is hard to define, it is a valuable asset for a Corporate Curator. In addition, it is important for the aspiring Curator to have a strong ability to communicate with very different people—both artists and corporate executives, for example.

Organizations and Associations

The organization for Corporate Curators is the Association of Professional Art Advisors (see Appendix IV).

Tips for Entry

Any experience in registrar work—perhaps volunteering in a local museum—will be helpful in gaining entry to this field.

ART CONSULTANT

Duties: Keep current on art trends; establish contacts with artists, galleries and clients; market consulting services

Alternate Titles: None

Salary Range: $8,000 to $100,000

Employment Prospects: Fair

Advancement Prospects: Poor

Prerequisites:

Education—No degree required, but most have college degrees

Experience—Extensive familiarity with the art world; art gallery experience is especially useful

Special Skills—Sales skills, organizational ability, outgoing nature

```
┌─────────────────────────┐
│                         │
│     Art Consultant      │
│                         │
└─────────────────────────┘

┌─────────────────────────┐
│                         │
│     Gallery Position    │
│                         │
└─────────────────────────┘
```

Position Description

An Art Consultant is a person, usually self-employed, who assists people in buying artwork. Because buying art can be an important investment, and because the art world seems complex and unfamiliar to some people, potential art buyers may wish to call on the services of someone who is more familiar with various kinds of artwork, artists and galleries to help them make a purchase decision.

Generally, Art Consultants have had a lifelong interest in art and spend a great deal of time and energy learning about different styles and trends in the art world. They may have majored in art or art history in college. They may have volunteered or been employed by a local art museum. They may have worked in one or more art galleries. Most typically, art is both an occupation and a hobby for them, and as Art Consultants they find enjoyment in bringing their own love of art to others.

To get started, one may go to work for one of the few large art consulting firms. Such firms generally work on a contract basis to assist corporations in decorating their offices with art, or to help builders to design art into their new office complexes to make them more attractive. In such a consulting firm one can get a good feel for the business and for the delicate skills needed to match art to a client's taste.

Alternatively, someone with experience in gallery or museum work and a large number of potential clients can go into business for him or herself as an Art Consultant. Such a person would select galleries and artists with whom to work, creating a good mix of styles and prices, and then go about attracting clients. The Consultant may initiate monthly events, such as bus tours to nearby museums, visits to artists' studios or lectures at certain galleries. He or she will publicize these events through regular mailings to a client list. Compensation will come from commissions on gallery purchases by clients and/or flat fees on top of the price of clients' purchases directly from artists.

Salaries

A self-employed Consultant can earn from $8,000 to $100,000 a year, depending on the number and size of his or her clients. A Consultant who is employed by a large art consulting firm will earn from $15,000 to $30,000.

Employment Prospects

It is fairly easy to obtain employment with an art consulting firm if you have a degree in art or art history and some sales and interpersonal skills. To be an independent Art Consultant, you must have extensive contacts in the art world and some start-up capital.

Advancement Prospects

Independent Consultants generally view this work as a lifelong goal, and few wish to advance beyond it. Increased earnings may thus be viewed as a kind of advancement. Art Consultants working for consulting firms have limited opportunities for advancement, and they may wish to go out on their own as Consultants or to move into gallery work.

Education

Art consulting firms generally require bachelor's degrees, and most independent Consultants have such degrees as well.

Experience and Skills

There are no specific requirements, but any experience in gallery or museum work will be useful. Sales and marketing experience is helpful as well.

A successful Art Consultant is likely to have spent a great deal of free time learning about art through such means as lectures, courses, talking to artists and poking around museums. The more outgoing and curious one is, and the more contacts he or she has in the art world, the better his or her chances of success.

Organizations and Associations

An Art Consultant should be a member of any art museum in his or her area.

Tips for Entry

This is a job in which volunteer work at a museum can be helpful. Giving tours, helping to arrange lectures, assisting curators—anything that increases your knowledge of art and your contacts within the art world—will help prepare you for working as an Art Consultant.

ART TRANSPORTER

CAREER PROFILE

Duties: Coordinating traveling art exhibits; consolidating works; overseeing transportation arrangements; liaison with lenders, institutions and local carriers

Alternate Title: Traffic Manager

Salary Range: $16,000 to $25,000

Employment Prospects: Good

Advancement Prospects: Good

Prerequisites:

    Education—Bachelor's degree in art or art history, with some business coursework

    Experience—Exposure to transportation and freight industry

    Special Skills—Administrative ability, detail orientation, typing

CAREER LADDER

```
+--------------------------------+
|                                |
|     Sales Representative        |
|                                |
+--------------------------------+

+--------------------------------+
|                                |
|     Art Transporter             |
|                                |
+--------------------------------+

+--------------------------------+
|                                |
|     Warehouse Manager           |
|                                |
+--------------------------------+
```

Position Description

An Art Transporter is a key person in the moving of artwork for exhibition—an important and growing aspect of the art and museum worlds. Art transportation includes the packing, shipping and tracking of individual pieces of art; it is a specialized business because of the value of the goods being transported and the special care the works require. But a major part of the art transportation business is the coordination of the moving of entire exhibits from city to city and museum to museum, often over great distances and lengthy periods of time.

The Art Transporter is responsible for the smooth movement of such exhibits. The Art Transporter deals with museum registrars, local freight carriers, lenders of artwork, and others, in the consolidation, packing, dispatching and moving of works. As a traffic manager, the Art Transporter will be given a complete itinerary for an exhibit before it begins and will be responsible for monitoring all the details of its delivery to each museum in a timely fashion.

Salaries

Art Transporters can expect to start at around $16,000 per year. Those with more experience and those who work for larger art transportation firms can make up to $25,000 per year.

Employment Prospects

Art transportation is a fairly open field in which to find employment, especially for someone who is willing to start at the bottom and work up. Because the field is not well known to the public, competition for positions is less intense than in other art-related careers.

Advancement Prospects

Chances for advancement in art transportation are good, particularly for those who wish to move into the sales area. There are frequent openings for representatives to sell art transportation services to galleries and museums; experience in traffic management will enable a sales-oriented person to make an easy transition into an outside sales position.

Education

A bachelor's degree in art or art history is good preparation for a career in art transportation. Business courses should supplement the liberal arts or fine arts background in order to provide some practical training.

Experience and Skills

The best possible practical experience for someone wishing to enter this field is to work with a van transportation or air freight business. Familiarity with transportation procedures—and, in particular, with bills of lading—is valuable to potential employers in this business.

A detail orientation is important for the successful Art Transporter, who may have to track several important exhibits. Any business, administrative or commercial skills will be valuable. Typing is an important skill for an art transporter, and he or she should be articulate in order to deal effectively with museum personnel, art lenders, freight carriers and others.

This is a deadline-oriented, high-pressure business, and the ability to deal with stress is valuable to those working in it.

Tips for Entry

Art transportation is a business in which one can truly work up the ladder. Full- or part-time warehouse work can lead to on-the-job training for a career in this business. In addition, any contacts with museum registrars and/or fine art packers would be useful.

FRAMING TECHNICIAN

CAREER PROFILE

Duties: Cutting, mounting, joining, blocking, stretching and assembling framing materials

Alternate Title: Framing Apprentice

Salary Range: $8,000 to $16,000

Employment Prospects: Good

Advancement Prospects: Good

Prerequisites:

Education—High school; may be a part-time job for high school student

Experience—None

Special Skills—Manual dexterity, eye for design

CAREER LADDER

```
┌─────────────────────────────┐
│                             │
│    Framing Salesperson      │
│                             │
└─────────────────────────────┘

┌─────────────────────────────┐
│                             │
│     Framing Technician      │
│                             │
└─────────────────────────────┘

┌─────────────────────────────┐
│                             │
│          Student            │
│                             │
└─────────────────────────────┘
```

Position Description

A Framing Technician is the junior employee of a frame shop. He or she is in a training position in which all the skills of framing are learned. The Technician will become familiar with the materials used in framing and the methods by which a frame is assembled.

Under the supervision of a framer, the Technician will learn to cut glass, mats and frames; how to block, stretch and dry-mount materials that are to be framed; how to join frames; and how to assemble the various materials for a completed frame.

Once these skills have been learned, the Technician will execute the frame designs created by the salespeople in the frame shop. It is expected that the Technician will work with care and that he or she will have some understanding of the design elements of the custom frame.

Salaries

The Framing Technician usually works for an hourly wage that ranges from $4.00 for a beginner to $6.00 for more experienced personnel.

Employment Prospects

It is fairly easy to obtain a position as a Frame Technician. This entry-level job is a good part-time occupation for a high school or college student who is taking art courses.

Advancement Prospects

A Frame Technician who learns quickly and performs diligently has a good chance of being promoted to framing salesperson.

Education

A high school diploma is a general requirement for a Framing Technician, but a high school student may be hired for this position on a part-time or vacation basis.

Experience and Skills

No particular experience is necessary, but a background in art is helpful. This is a training position in which most of the skills of the trade will be learned, but manual dexterity and the ability to work carefully and plan ahead are valuable. An instinct for design would be useful as well.

Organizations and Associations

The Professional Picture Framers Association (see Appendix IV) serves people in this field.

Tips for Entry

Check with all the frame shops in your area, and be persistent. Your eagerness to learn could be valuable to a potential employer.

FRAMING SALESPERSON

CAREER PROFILE

Duties: Assisting customers in selecting custom framing; preparing and assembling custom frames; training framing technicians

Alternate Title: Senior Framing Technician

Salary Range: $14,000 to $16,000

Employment Prospects: Good

Advancement Prospects: Fair

Prerequisites:

Education—High school; art background; framing apprenticeship

Experience—Work in frame shop

Special Skills—Framing skills

CAREER LADDER

```
┌─────────────────────────────┐
│       Custom Framer         │
└─────────────────────────────┘

┌─────────────────────────────┐
│    Framing Salesperson      │
└─────────────────────────────┘

┌─────────────────────────────┐
│      Frame Technician       │
└─────────────────────────────┘
```

Position Description

Framing Salespeople are the helpful counter people at a frame shop. They assist customers by displaying various framing materials and making suggestions as to the design of a custom frame.

This is a challenging position, because customers bring a wide variety of items in for framing, and the Salesperson must try to help the customer create a frame that will suit both the artwork and the environment in which it will eventually be displayed. This is a matter of taste and design, and the Salesperson must learn when to lend his or her expertise and when to tactfully bow to the customer's preferences. Thus, this job requires design skills, knowledge of the materials available, communications ability and the technical framing skills to bring it all together.

The Framing Salesperson is also responsible for writing orders carefully and correctly, so that the frame will be assembled properly, and for calculating the price of the finished frame. In addition, the Salesperson may have to instruct or assist one or more technicians in constructing frames.

Salaries

Framing Salespeople are usually paid by the hour, generally in a range from $6.00 to $8.00.

Employment Prospects

It is relatively easy for a framer with some experience to get a job as a Framing Salesperson. There are many frame shops, and turnover is fairly high.

Advancement Prospects

Advancement from this position is only fair. To advance, one may become a frame shop manager, a job in which there is considerably less turnover. Or a Framing Salesperson may open his or her own frame shop, which requires capital and some business administration skills.

Education

A high school diploma is generally required, and a framing apprenticeship is a must. This is not an entry-level position.

Experience and Skills

A Framing Salesperson should have one to two years of experience as a framing technician. It is necessary for a Framing Salesperson to have a full range of framing skills, which are usually acquired through an informal framing apprenticeship.

Organizations and Associations

Framing salespersons may wish to join the Professional Picture Framers Association (see Appendix IV).

Tips for Entry

It is often possible to obtain employment as a Framing Salesperson on a part-time basis. This can lead to full-time employment later.

CUSTOM FRAMER

CAREER PROFILE

Duties: Managing frame shop, designing frame jobs, hiring, training, sales

Alternate Titles: Framer, Frame Shop/Gallery Manager

Salary Range: $20,000 to $35,000

Employment Prospects: Fair

Advancement Prospects: Poor

Prerequisites:

Education—Art background; bachelor's degree helpful; business courses useful

Experience—Framing apprenticeship; sales; business administration

Special Skills—Framing skills

CAREER LADDER

```
┌─────────────────────────────┐
│      Custom Framer          │
└─────────────────────────────┘

┌─────────────────────────────┐
│    Framing Salesperson      │
└─────────────────────────────┘
```

Position Description

The Custom Framer manages a store that specializes in custom frame work. Many such stores also house small galleries, with which the Custom Framer may be involved. In general, however, the Custom Framer is responsible for assisting customers in selecting framing materials, designing the framing, and executing the framing or directing others to do so.

The framer hires and trains sales clerks, designers and technicians to assist him or her in performing these tasks. He or she will be involved in business administration activities as well, such as bookkeeping, advertising and purchasing of materials.

Some Custom Framers own their own shops; others manage such shops for their owners. Store owners are generally more involved with the business aspects of the shop than are Custom Framers, who are usually working for others. A frame shop owner may see this entrepreneurial position as his or her ultimate goal, not wishing to advance further. A Custom Framer who is working for somebody else is unlikely to advance unless he or she opens a frame shop of his or her own.

Salaries

Salaries for people in this position range from about $20,000 for the manager of a small frame shop to about $35,000 for the person who manages a larger shop. The owner of a custom frame shop may make more than this if the store is especially profitable.

Employment Prospects

It is fairly easy for someone who has served a framing apprenticeship to become a Custom Framer once he or she has some experience. There are many frame shops, and experienced personnel are hard to find. For an owner, it requires capital to start up or purchase a framing business.

Advancement Prospects

Custom Framers find it difficult to advance in the field without opening their own businesses. An owner may consider advancement to mean increased profitability of his or her business.

Education

A high school diploma is a standard requirement; an art background is helpful, and any business courses would be useful.

Experience and Skills

A Custom Framer should have several years of experience in framing. It is necessary for a Custom

Framer to have served an apprenticeship in framing. This is not a formal program, but a period of training in mounting, cutting, blocking, stretching, joining and designing of framing materials. Most Framers acquire this training by working in sales and technician positions at frame shops.

Organizations and Associations

A Custom Framer may wish to join the Professional Picture Framers Association (see Appendix IV).

Tips for Entry

Any employment experience in a frame shop—even part-time—will be useful.

ART SUPPLY SALESPERSON

CAREER PROFILE

Duties: Assist customers, take inventory, reorder items, make sales

Alternate Title: Art Supply Salesclerk

Salary Range: $3.50 per hour to $5.00 per hour

Employment Prospects: Good

Advancement Prospects: Good

Prerequisites:
   Education—High school diploma

   Experience—None

   Special Skills—Dependability, honesty, willingness to learn and to work hard, friendliness

CAREER LADDER

```
┌─────────────────────────────┐
│                             │
│   Art Supply Store Manager  │
│                             │
└─────────────────────────────┘

┌─────────────────────────────┐
│                             │
│   Art Supply Salesperson    │
│                             │
└─────────────────────────────┘

┌─────────────────────────────┐
│                             │
│          Student            │
│                             │
└─────────────────────────────┘
```

Position Description

An Art Supply Salesperson is the customer contact person in an art supply store. The job's duties include helping customers to find the items they need; assisting customers with information about art supplies; ringing up sales; inventorying items in the store; reordering items as needed; and performing other tasks the manager may require, such as stocking shelves or dusting merchandise.

An art supply store usually has one or more Salespersons working for a store manager. Hours generally follow the normal retail times, with some evening hours available, as well as weekend hours.

Salaries

Most Art Supply Salespersons are paid on an hourly basis, with rates running from $3.50 to $5.00 per hour. A full-time Salesperson would earn about $7,500 to $10,000 a year.

Employment Prospects

There are good opportunities for young people to get into this job. Many high school and college students find part-time work in art supply stores.

Advancement Prospects

The chances for advancement in this field are good. A hardworking, capable employee can work his or her way up to become an assistant store manager or a store manager.

Education

There is no particular educational requirement for Art Supply Salespeople. A high school or college student can qualify for this position.

Experience and Skills

Most store managers are willing to hire inexperienced people for this job, but they generally prefer people with some previous experience in sales.

Personal qualities are more important than experience for a beginning Art Supply Salesperson. It is imperative that the Salesperson be dependable and honest. Friendliness and courteousness are key attributes. Finally, a willingness to learn and to work hard is valuable to potential employers.

Tips for Entry

Though there are no special educational requirements for this job, any art courses and business courses—high school or college—will be beneficial.

ART SUPPLY STORE MANAGER

CAREER PROFILE

Duties: Supervise employees, handle accounting, assist customers, oversee advertising, order merchandise

Alternate Titles: None

Salary Range: $12,000 to $25,000

Employment Prospects: Good

Advancement Prospects: Poor

Prerequisites:

Education—Bachelor's degree preferred

Experience—Previous sales experience

Special Skills—Organization, detail orientation, management ability, sales skills

CAREER LADDER

```
┌─────────────────────────────────┐
│                                 │
│    Art Supply Store Manager     │
│                                 │
└─────────────────────────────────┘

┌─────────────────────────────────┐
│                                 │
│      Art Supply Salesperson     │
│                                 │
└─────────────────────────────────┘
```

Position Description

An Art Supply Store Manager is responsible for the smooth functioning of an art supply store. This includes the hiring and training of employees; ordering merchandise and monitoring sales; handling or overseeing the bookkeeping and accounting; making sure the store is clean and orderly; and performing the same customer assistance and sales duties as the art supply salespeople.

The Manager should be prepared to work long hours, since he or she cannot normally perform all of these functions between nine and five. Evening and weekend work are usually required to keep the store running smoothly.

Salaries

Salaries for Art Supply Store Managers generally range from $12,000 to $25,000 per year.

Employment Prospects

There are good opportunities for people with experience in this field to move up to store management. Since there is high turnover on the salesclerk level, there is limited competition for management positions.

Advancement Prospects

Opportunities to advance in this field are poor. Store management is the highest position available, though an individual may wish to open his or her own store or to find work with an art supply manufacturer.

Education

Not all art supply stores require their Managers to have college degrees, but such degrees are helpful.

Experience and Skills

Art Supply Store Managers should have previous experience as art supply salespersons. In addition, an art background and familiarity with art supplies is important.

The Store Manager should have supervisory skills, general business and sales skills, and such qualities as dependability, honesty, willingness to work hard and friendliness.

Organizations and Associations

The organization for the art supply business is the National Art Materials Trade Association (see Appendix IV).

Tips for Entry

The combination of experience in business and in art is valuable to employers in this field.

SECTION 9
APPENDIXES

APPENDIX I

EDUCATIONAL INSTITUTIONS

The great majority of colleges and universities offer degree programs in art and art history, so we have not listed them here; a general college guide such as *Lovejoy's* or *Barron's* will provide you with listings of these common majors. However, programs of study in art therapy, art conservation and arts administration or arts management are less common; the listing is presented here to make the information more readily accessible.

ART THERAPY

CALIFORNIA

Immaculate Heart College
2021 N. Western Ave.
Los Angeles, CA 90027
(213) 462-1301

U.S. International University
10455 Pomerado Rd.
San Diego, CA 92131
(619) 271-4300

CONNECTICUT

Albertus Magnus College
700 Prospect St.
New Haven, CT 06511
(203) 773-8550

DISTRICT OF COLUMBIA

George Washington University
Washington, DC 20052
(202) 676-6040

ILLINOIS

Barat College
700 E. Westleigh Rd.
Lake Forest, IL 60045
(312) 234-3000

Eureka College
300 E. College Ave.
Eureka, IL 61530
(309) 467-3721

Millikin University
1184 W. Main St.
Decatur, IL 62522
(217) 424-6210

School of the Art Institute of Chicago
Columbus Drive & Jackson Blvd.
Chicago, IL 60603
(312) 443-3710

University of Illinois—Chicago
801 S. Morgan
Chicago, IL 60680
(312) 996-0998

INDIANA

Indiana Central University
1400 E. Hanna Ave.
Indianapolis, IN 46227
(317) 788-3216

University of Evansville
Evansville, IN 47702
(812) 479-2468

KANSAS

Emporia State University
1200 Commercial St.
Emporia, KS 66801
(316) 343-1200

Pittsburg State University
1701 S. Broadway
Pittsburg, KS 66762
(316) 231-7000

KENTUCKY

University of Louisville
2301 S. 3rd St.
Louisville, KY 40208
(502) 588-5555

MARYLAND

Goucher College
Baltimore, MD 21204
(301) 337-6100

MASSACHUSETTS

Lesley College
29 Everett St.
Cambridge, MA 02138
(617) 868-9600

MISSOURI

Maryville College—St. Louis
13550 Conway Rd.
St. Louis, MO 63141
(314) 434-4100

Northeast Missouri State University
E. Normal St.
Kirksville, MO 63501
(816) 785-4114

NEW JERSEY

Burlington County College
Pemberton-Browns Mills Rd.
Pemberton, NJ 08068
(609) 893-4005

Trenton State College
Pennington Rd.
Box 940
Hillwood Lakes
Trenton, NJ 08625
(609) 771-2131

NEW YORK

College of New Rochelle
Castle Pl.
New Rochelle, NY 10801
(914) 632-5300

Long Island University, C.W. Post Center
Greenvale, NY 11548
(516) 299-0200

New York University
25 W. 4th St.
New York, NY 10012
(212) 598-3591

Pratt Institute
200 Willoughby Ave.
Brooklyn, NY 11205
(718) 636-7365

Russell Sage College
51 First St.
Troy, NY 12180
(518) 270-2217

OHIO

Columbus College of Art & Design
47 N. Washington Ave.
Columbus, OH 43215
(614) 224-9101

Ohio University
120 Chubb Hall
Athens, OH 45701
(614) 594-5174

Wright State University
Colonel Glenn Hwy.
Dayton, OH 45435
(513) 873-2211

PENNSYLVANIA

Beaver College
Easton & Church Rds.
Glenside, PA 19038
(215) 572-2900

Hahnemann University
230 N. Broad St.
Philadelphia, PA 10102
(215) 448-7000

Marywood College
2300 Adams Ave.
Scranton, PA 18509
(717) 348-6234

Mercyhurst College
Glenwood Hills
Erie, PA 16546
(814) 825-0200

St. Vincent College
Latrobe, PA 15650
(412) 539-9761

Seton Hill College
Greensburg, PA 15601
(412) 838-4255

TEXAS

Baylor University
Waco, TX 76798
(817) 755-3985

VERMONT

Vermont College of Norwich University
Montpelier, VT 05602
(802) 229-0522

WEST VIRGINIA

Salem College
223 W. Main St.
Salem, WV 26426
(304) 782-5336

Shepherd College
Shepherdstown, WV 25443
(304) 876-2511

WISCONSIN

Alverno College
3401 S. 39th St.
Milwaukee, WI 53215
(414) 647-3700

Mount Mary College
2900 Menomonee River Parkway
Milwaukee, WI 53222
(414) 259-9220

ART CONSERVATION

DELAWARE

Winterthur/University of Delaware Program in the Conservation of Artistic and Historic Works
301 Old College
University of Delaware
Newark, DE 19711

NEW YORK

Conservation Center, Institute of Fine Arts
New York University
Chan House
14 E. 78th St.
New York, NY 10021

State University College at Buffalo
Art Conservation Department
PO Box 71
Cooperstown, NY 13326

ARTS ADMINISTRATION

CALIFORNIA

Golden State University
536 Mission St.
San Francisco, CA 94105
(415) 442-7000

INDIANA

Indiana University—Bloomington
Bloomington, IN 47401
(812) 335-0661

MASSACHUSETTS

Simmons College
300 The Fenway
Boston, MA 02115
(617) 738-2107

MINNESOTA

Saint Cloud State University
First Ave. S.
St. Cloud, MN 56301
(612) 255-0121

NORTH CAROLINA

Pfeiffer College
Misenheimer, NC 28109
(704) 463-7343

TEXAS

Southern Methodist University
PO Box 296
Dallas, TX 75275
(214) 692-2058

University of Texas—Austin
Austin, TX 78712
(512) 471-1711

WISCONSIN

University of Wisconsin—Madison
750 University Ave.
Madison, WI 53706
(608) 262-3961

Viterbo College
815 S. 9th St.
La Crosse, WI 54601
(608) 784-0040

ARTS MANAGEMENT

DISTRICT OF COLUMBIA

American University
440 Massachusetts & Nebraska Ave.
  NW
Washington, DC 20016
(202) 885-6000

FLORIDA

University of Tampa
401 W. Kennedy Blvd.
Tampa, FL 33606
(813) 253-3333

GEORGIA

Wesleyan College
4760 Forsyth Rd.
Macon, GA 31297
(912) 477-0115

ILLINOIS

Elmhurst College
190 Prospect Ave.
Elmhurst, IL 60126
(312) 279-4100

Eureka College
300 E. College Ave.
Eureka, IL 61530
(309) 467-3721

KANSAS

Ottawa University
10th & Cedar
Ottawa, KS 66067
(800) 255-6380

LOUISIANA

Northeast Louisiana University
700 University Ave.
Monroe, LA 71209
(318) 342-2011

MARYLAND

Goucher College
Baltimore, MD 21204
(301) 337-6100

MICHIGAN

Eastern Michigan University
Ypsilanti, MI 48197
(313) 487-1849

MISSOURI

Culver-Stockton College
Canton, MO 63435
(314) 288-5221

NEW YORK

**Long Island University, C.W. Post
  Center**
Greenvale, NY 11548
(516) 299-0200

Medaille College
18 Agassiz Circle
Buffalo, NY 14214
(716) 884-3281

Russell Sage College
51 First St.
Troy, NY 12180
(518) 270-2217

NORTH CAROLINA

Salem College
Salem Station
Winston-Salem, NC 27108
(919) 721-2621

OHIO

Baldwin-Wallace College
275 Eastland Rd.
Berea, OH 44017
(216) 826-2900

Lake Erie College
391 W. Washington St.
Painesville, OH 44077
(216) 352-3361

PENNSYLVANIA

Carlow College
3333 5th Ave.
Pittsburgh, PA 15213
(412) 578-6000

VIRGINIA

Mary Baldwin College
Frederick St.
Staunton, VA 24401
(703) 887-7000

Randolph Macon College
Ashland, VA 23005
(804) 798-8372

APPENDIX II

TRADE, INDUSTRIAL AND VOCATIONAL SCHOOLS

The following is a list of schools that offer training in art—generally career-oriented and geared to aspiring commercial, graphic and fine artists. They range from public vocational high schools and community colleges to private instructional studios and profit-making trade schools.

ALABAMA

Bessemer State Technical College
PO Box 308
Bessemer, AL 35020
(205) 428-6391

Jefferson County Vocational School
Route 15
Box 205
Birmingham, AL 35224

Missy's Fine Arts Studio
1301 5th St. W.
Jasper, AL 35501

ALASKA

Alaska Pacific University
4101 University Dr.
Anchorage, AK 99508
(907) 561-1266

Anchorage International Art Institute
3005 Wendy's Way
Anchorage, AK 99503
(907) 274-0732

Career Center
2650 E. Northern Lights Blvd.
Anchorage, AK 99508
(907) 278-9631

Ketchikan Community College
7th & Madison
Ketchikan, AK 99901

Sheldon Jackson College
PO Box 479
Sitka, AK 99835
(907) 747-6284

Sitka Community College
PO Box 1090
Sitka, AK 99835

ARIZONA

Kachina Schools, Inc.
3801 N. 30th St.
Phoenix, AZ 85016
(602) 955-5930

Maricopa Technical Community College
108 N. 40th St.
Phoenix, AZ 85034
(602) 275-8500

Mohave Community College
1971 Jagerson Ave.
Kingman, AZ 86401
(602) 757-4331

ARKANSAS

Arkansas Arts Center
PO Box 2137
Little Rock, AR 72203

Southwest Vocational-Technical Institute
PO Box 45
East Camden, AR 71701

CALIFORNIA

Academy of Art College
540 Powell St.
San Francisco, CA 94108
(415) 673-4200

Alexander School of Painting
2068 Front St.
San Diego, CA 92101
(619) 234-7356

Allan Hancock College
800 S. College Dr.
Santa Maria, CA 93454
(805) 922-6966

Butte Community College
Route 1
Box 183 A
Oroville, CA 95965
(916) 895-2511

Carmel Art Institute
PO Box 9
Carmel, CA 93921

College of the Canyons
26455 N. Rockwell Canyon Rd.
Valencia, CA 91355
(805) 259-7800

Columbia College
PO Box 1849
Columbia, CA 95310
(209) 532-3141

Continental Schools
1330 W. Olympia Blvd.
Los Angeles, CA 90015
(213) 381-6627

Foothill College
12345 El Monte Rd.
Los Altos Hills, CA 94022
(415) 948-8590

Hemphill Schools
1543 W. Olympic Blvd.
Suite 226
Los Angeles, CA 90015
(213) 381-1898

Hollywood Art Center School
2025-2027 N. Highland Ave.
Los Angeles, CA 90028
(213) 851-1103

Los Angeles County Art Institute
2401 Wilshire Blvd.
Los Angeles, CA 90057

Merritt College
12500 Campus Dr.
Oakland, CA 94619
(415) 436-2482

Mount San Antonio College
1100 N. Grand Ave.
Walnut, CA 91789
(714) 594-5611

Mount San Jacinto College
21400 Highway 79
San Jacinto, CA 92383
(714) 654-8011

Pacific Institute of Commercial Art
2333 W. 3rd St.
Los Angeles, CA 90057
(213) 388-5669

Rancho Santiago Community College District
17th & Bristol St.
Santa Ana, CA 92706
(714) 667-3000

Richmond Art Center
25th & Barrett
Richmond, CA 94804

San Bernardino Valley College
701 S. Mt. Vernon Ave.
San Bernardino, CA 92410
(714) 888-6511

San Diego City College
1313 12th Ave.
San Diego, CA 92101
(619) 230-2400

San Francisco Art Institute
800 Chestnut St.
San Francisco, CA 94133
(415) 771-7020

Southwestern College
900 Otay Lakes Rd.
Chula Vista, CA 92010
(619) 421-6700

COLORADO

Arapahoe-Douglas Area Vocational School
5833 S. Prince
Littleton, CO 80120

Art Center Institute
1326 S. Elizabeth St.
Denver, CO 80210

Aurora Public Schools Technical Center
500 Buckley Rd.
Aurora, CO 80011

Community College of Denver
Auraria Campus
111 W. Colfax Ave.
Denver, CO 80204
(303) 466-8811

Mesa College Area Vocational School
PO Box 2647
Grand Junction, CO 81501
(303) 248-1514

Pikes Peak Community College
5675 S. Academy Blvd.
Colorado Springs, CO 80906
(303) 576-7711

Rocky Mountain School of Art
1441 Ogden St.
Denver, CO 80218
(303) 832-1557

University of Denver School of Art
University Park Station
Denver, CO 80210

CONNECTICUT

Art Guild
Church St.
Farmington, CT 06032
(203) 677-6205

Connecticut Institute of Art & Design
1080 Silas Deane Hwy.
Hartford, CT 06109
(203) 563-8156

Hartford Art School
University of Hartford
200 Bloomfield Ave.
Hartford, CT 06117

Paier College of Art
6 Prospect Court
New Haven, CT 06511
(203) 777-3851

Propersi School of Art, Inc.
581 W. Putnam Ave.
Greenwich, CT 06830
(203) 869-4430

DELAWARE

Delaware Art Museum School
2301 Kentmere Pky.
Wilmington, DE 19806

DISTRICT OF COLUMBIA

Corcoran School of Art
17th & New York Ave. NW
Washington, DC 20006
(202) 628-9484

FLORIDA

Art Center Workshop, Inc.
1401 B N. Federal Hwy.
Fort Lauderdale, FL 33304
(305) 565-5951

Bauder College
4801 N. Dixie Hwy.
Fort Lauderdale, FL 33334
(305) 491-7171

Broward Community College
225 E. Las Olas Blvd.
Fort Lauderdale, FL 33301
(305) 761-7400

Dixie Hollins Evening Adult Education Center
4940 62nd St. N.
St. Petersburg, FL 33709

Dunedin Fine Arts & Cultural Center
1143 Michigan Blvd.
Dunedin, FL 33528
(813) 736-6731

Florida Keys Community College
1 Junior College Rd.
Key West, FL 33040
(305) 296-9081

Fort Lauderdale Adult Education Center
1600 NE 4th Ave.
Fort Lauderdale, FL 33305

Haney Area Vocational-Technical Center
3016 Highway 77
Panama City, FL 32405
(904) 769-3315

Lindsey Hopkins Education Center
1410 NE 2nd Ave.
Miami, FL 33132

Lively Vocational-Technical Center
6410 Orient Rd.
Tampa, FL 33610
(904) 576-3181

Martin Technical College
1901 NW 7th St.
Miami, FL 33125
(305) 541-8140

McMurrough School of Art
735 S. Robin Way
Satellite Beach, FL 32937

Miami Adult Education Center
2450 SW 1st St.
Miami, FL 33135

Miami-Dade Community College
11011 SW 104th St.
Miami, FL 33176

**Miami Lakes Technical Education
Center**
5780 NW 158th St.
Miami, FL 33014
(305) 557-1100

**Miami Lake/Tomlinson Adult Education
Center**
709 Mirror Lake Dr. N.
St. Petersburg, FL 33701
(813) 821-4593

North Miami Museum & Art Center
12340 NE 8th Ave.
North Miami, FL 33161

Ringling School of Art
1191 27th St.
Sarasota, FL 33580

**St. Petersburg Vocational-Technical
Institute**
901 34th St. So.
St. Petersburg, FL 33711
(813) 327-3671

South Florida Art Institute
1301 S. Ocean Dr.
Hollywood, FL 33019
(305) 923-6490

South Technical Education Center
1300 SW 30th Ave.
Boynton Beach, FL 33435

**Tampa Bay Area Vocational-Technical
Center**
6410 Orient Rd.
Tampa, FL 33610
(813) 621-2441

Tampa Technical Institute Campus
3920 E. Hillsborough Ave.
Tampa, FL 33610
(813) 238-0455

Westside Vocational Skills Center
7450 Wilson Blvd.
Jacksonville, FL 32210
(904) 778-7212

GEORGIA

Atlanta School of Art
1280 Peachtree St. NE
Atlanta, GA 30309
(404) 873-1701

Herbert Memorial Institute of Art
506 Telfair St.
Augusta, GA 96814

HAWAII

Foss School of Fine Arts, Ltd.
PO Box 3071
Honolulu, HI 96820
(808) 839-1573

Honolulu Academy of Arts
900 S. Beretania St.
Honolulu, HI 96814

ILLINOIS

American Academy of Art
220 S. State St.
Chicago, IL 60604
(312) 939-3883

Art Institute of Chicago
Michigan Ave. & Adams St.
Chicago, IL 60601
(312) 443-3700

Contemporary Art Workshop
542 W. Grant Pl.
Chicago, IL 60614

La Salle Extension University
3004 Glenview Rd.
Wilmette, IL 60091

Peoria Art Guild
1831 N. Knoxville Rd.
Peoria, IL 61603
(309) 685-7522

Richard J. Daley College
7500 S. Pulaski Rd.
Chicago, IL 60652

Thornton Community College
15800 S. State St.
South Holland, IL 60473

Wilbur Wright College
3400 N. Austin Ave.
Chicago, IL 60625
(312) 878-1550

INDIANA

J. Everett Light Career Center
1901 E. 86th St.
Indianapolis, IN 46240

Tucker Area Career Center
State Road 18 & Pennsylvania
Marion, IN 46952
(317) 662-2546

IOWA

Des Moines Art Center School
4700 Grand Ave.
Des Moines, IA 50312
(515) 277-4405

Des Moines Technical High School
18th & Grand
Des Moines, IA 50307

Hawkeye Institue of Technology
1501 E. Orange Rd.
Waterloo, IA 50704
(319) 296-3120

KANSAS

Highland Community College
Highland, KS 66035

Johnson County Community College
111th & Quivira Rd.
Shawnee Mission, KS 66210

**Kansas City, Kansas Community
College**
7250 State Ave.
Kansas City, KS 66122

**Northeast Kansas Area Vocational-
Technical School**
PO Box 277
Atchison, KS 66002

Pratt Community College
Highway 61
Pratt, KS 67124

Wichita Art Association School of Art
9112 E. Central
Wichita, KS 67206
(316) 686-6687

LOUISIANA

Cameron College
2740 Canal St.
New Orleans, LA 70119
(504) 821-5881

New Orleans Art Institute
6055 Magazine St.
New Orleans, LA 70118
(504) 899-2081

Southern Technical College
3081 Ambassador Caffery
Lafayette, LA 70503
(318) 981-4010

Sowela Technical Institute
3820 Legion St.
Lake Charles, LA 70616
(318) 491-2688

MAINE

Portland School of Art
97 Spring
Portland, ME 04111
(207) 775-3052

MARYLAND

Baltimore Art Institute
2 Sherwood Ave.
Baltimore, MD 21208
(301) 484-7992

Carver Vocational-Technical School
2201 Presstman
Baltimore, MD 21216

Hagerstown Junior College
751 Robinwood Dr.
Hagerstown, MD 21740

Le Millet Private Art School
2415 St. Paul St.
Baltimore, MD 21218
(301) 665-7636

Maryland School of Art
10500 Georgia Ave.
Silver Spring, MD 20902
(301) 649-4454

Mergenthaler Vocational-Technical School
3500 Hillen Rd.
Baltimore, MD 21218

Professional Institute of Commercial Art
4020 Clarks La.
Baltimore, MD 21215
(301) 358-6311

Salisbury State College
Camden Ave.
Salisbury, MD 21801

Schuler School of Fine Arts
5 E. Lafayette Ave.
Baltimore, MD 21202
(301) 685-3568

Southeastern Vocational-Technical Center
325 Sollers Pt. Rd.
Baltimore, MD 21222

MASSACHUSETTS

Art Institute of Boston
700 Beacon St.
Boston, MA 02215
(617) 262-1223

Berkshire Community College
2nd St.
Pittsfield, MA 01201

Blue Hills Technical Institute
100 Randolph St.
Canton, MA 02021
(617) 828-5800

Butera School of Art
111 Beacon St.
Boston, MA 02116
(617) 536-4623

Cambridge Art Association
23 Garden
Cambridge, MA 02128

George Vesper School of Art
44 St. Botolph St.
Boston, MA 02116
(617) 267-2045

Greenfield Community College
125 Federal St.
Greenfield, MA 01301

Montserrat School of Visual Art
PO Box 62
Beverly, MA 01915
(617) 922-8222

Museum of Fine Arts School
230 Fenway St.
Boston, MA 02115

New England School of Art & Design
28 Newbury St.
Boston, MA 02216
(617) 536-0383

Newton Arts Center
61 Washington Park
Newtonville, MA 02160

North Shore Regional Vocational School District
20 Balch St.
Beverly, MA 01915

Whittier Regional Vocational-Technical High School
115 Amesbury Line Rd.
Haverhill, MA 01830

MICHIGAN

Art School of the Society of Arts & Crafts
245 E. Kirby
Detroit, MI 48202
(313) 872-3118

Kendall School of Design
1110 College Ave. NE
Grand Rapids, MI 49503
(616) 451-2787

Macomb County Community College
14500 Twelve Mile Rd.
Warren, MI 48093

Madonna College
36600 Schoolcraft Rd.
Livonia, MI 48150

Oakland Community College
Orchard Ridge Campus
Farmington, MI 48024

St. Clair County Community College
323 Erie St.
Port Huron, MI 48060

Washtenaw Community College
4800 E. Huron River Dr.
Ann Arbor, MI 48107

MINNESOTA

Area Vocational-Technical Institute
1600 Jefferson St.
Alexandria, MN 56308
(612) 762-0221

Area Vocational-Technical Institute
1920 Lee Blvd.
Mankato, MN 56001
(507) 625-3441

Art Instruction Schools, Inc.
500 S. 4th St.
Minneapolis, MN 55415
(612) 339-8721

Hennepin Technical Center
1820 N. Xenium La.
Plymouth, MN 55441

Minneapolis Technical Institute
1415 Hennepin Blvd.
Minneapolis, MN 55403
(612) 370-9400

North Hennepin Community College
7411 85th Ave. N.
Minneapolis, MN 55445
(612) 425-4541

St. Paul Area Vocational-Technical Institute
235 Marshall Ave.
St. Paul, MN 55102
(612) 221-1300

School of Associated Arts
344 Summit
St. Paul, MN 55102
(612) 224-3416

MISSOURI

Kansas City Art Institute & School of Design
4415 Warwick Blvd.
Kansas City, MO 64111
(816) 561-4852

Sikeston Area Vocational School
200 Pine St.
Sikeston, MO 63801
(314) 471-5440

NEBRASKA

Central Technical Community College
3134 W. Highway 34
Grand Island, NE 68802
(308) 384-5220

Metropolitan Technical Community College
30th & Fort St.
Omaha, NE 68110
(402) 449-8300

Platte Technical Community College
Box 1027
Columbus, NE 68601

Southeast Community College
Milford, NE 68405

Studio Academy School of Advertising Art & Design, Inc.
1021 N. 46th St.
Omaha, NE 68132
(402) 553-1733

NEVADA

Studio Workshop & Gallery
606-1/2 E. Sahara Ave.
Las Vegas, NV 89105

NEW HAMPSHIRE

Manchester Institute of Arts & Sciences
148 Concord St.
Manchester, NH 03104
(603) 669-2731

NEW JERSEY

Atlantic County Area Vocational-Technical School
Route 40 & 19th Ave.
Mays Landing, NJ 08330

Du Cret School of the Arts
1030 Central Ave.
Plainfield, NJ 07060
(201) 889-2000

Linden Area Vocational-Technical School
128 W. St. George Ave.
Linden, NJ 07036

Mercer County Vocational-Technical School
Assunpink Center
1085 Old Trenton Rd.
Trenton, NJ 08690
(609) 586-2121

Mercer County Vocational School
Sypek Center
129 Bull Run Rd.
Trenton, NJ 08638
(609) 883-8012

Middlesex County Area Vocational-Technical School
112 Rues La.
E. Brunswick, NJ 08816

Newark School of Fine & Industrial Art
550 King Blvd.
Newark, NJ 07102
(201) 733-7390

Passaic County Area Vocational-Technical School
45 Reinhardt Rd.
Wayne, NJ 07470

Union County Vocational Center
1776 Raritan Rd.
Scotch Plains, NJ 07076
(201) 889-2000

NEW MEXICO

Southwestern School of Art
10301 Comanche NE
Albuquerque, NM 87111
(505) 299-0316

NEW YORK

Albert Pels School of Art
226 W. 26th St.
New York, NY 10001
(212) 807-6686

Art Students League of New York
215 W. 57th St.
New York, NY 10019
(212) 247-4510

Broome Community College
Upper Front St.
Binghamton, NY 13902
(607) 771-5000

Catan-Rose Institute of Fine Arts
72-72 112th St.
Forest Hills, NY 11375
(718) 263-1962

Dutchess Community College
Pendell Rd.
Poughkeepsie, NY 12601

Lemily Studio School of Art
226 Jefferson St.
Albany, NY 12210
(518) 463-7774

National Academy School of Fine Art
5 E. 89th St.
New York, NY 10128
(212) 369-4880

New York Academy of Art
419 Lafayette St.
New York, NY 10003
(212) 505-5300

New York Studio School of Drawing, Painting & Sculpture
8 W. 8th St.
New York, NY 10011
(212) 673-6466

Parsons School of Design
66 5th Ave.
New York, NY 10011
(212) 741-8900

Queensboro Community College
56th Ave. & Springfield Blvd.
Bayside, NY 11364
(718) 631-6341

NORTH CAROLINA

Mint Museum of Art
PO Box 6011
Charlotte, NC 28207

Rutledge College of Winston-Salem
820 W. 4th St.
Winston-Salem, NC 27101
(919) 725-8701

Sawtooth Center for Visual Design
226 N. Marshall St.
Winston-Salem, NC 27101
(919) 723-7395

Technical College of Alamance
PO Box 623
Haw River, NC 27258
(919) 578-2002

NORTH DAKOTA

Bismarck Junior College
Schafer Heights, ND 58501
(701) 224-5400

OHIO

Academy of Communicative Art
2528 Kemper La.
Cincinnati, OH 45206
(513) 751-1206

Art Academy of Cincinnati
Eden Park
Cincinnati, OH 45202
(513) 721-5205

Art Advertising Academy
4343 Bridgetown Rd.
Cincinnati, OH 45211
(513) 574-1010

Ashtabula Art Center
2928 W. 13th
Ashtabula, OH 44004

Central Academy of Commercial Art
2326 Upland Pl.
Cincinnati, OH 45206
(513) 961-2484

Columbus College of Art & Design
47 N. Washington
Columbus, OH 43215
(614) 224-9101

Ohio Visual Art Institute
124 E. 7th St.
Cincinnati, OH 45202
(513) 241-4338

School of Fine Arts
38660 Mentor Ave.
Willoughby, OH 44094

OKLAHOMA

School of Art
Oklahoma Science & Arts Foundation
1300 N. Broadway
Oklahoma City, OK 73103

OREGON

Advertising Art School
924 SE 26th
Portland, OR 97214

Florence Thurman Studio of Art
4800 SW Maple
Beaverton, OR 97005

Museum Art School
1219 SW Park
Portland, OR 97205

Oregon College of Art
290 N. Main St.
Suite 1
Ashland, OR 97520

Southwest Oregon Community College
PO Box 509
Empire Station
Coos Bay, OR 97420
(503) 888-2525

PENNSYLVANIA

Altoona Area Vocational-Technical School
1500 4th Ave.
Altoona, PA 16602

Art Institute of New Kensington
401 9th St.
New Kensington, PA 15068

Art Institute of Philadelphia
1622 Chestnut St.
Philadelphia, PA 19103
(215) 567-7080

Art Institute of Pittsburgh
526 Penn Ave.
Pittsburgh, PA 15222
(412) 263-6600

Bok Area Vocational-Technical School
8th & Mifflin Sts.
Philadelphia, PA 19148

Brownstown Area Vocational-Technical School
PO Box 435
Brownstown, PA 17508

Frudakis Academy of Fine Arts
32 Strawberry St.
Philadelphia, PA 19106

Hussian School of Art
1010 Arch St.
Philadelphia, PA 19107
(215) 238-9000

Lancaster Area Vocational-Technical School
1730 Hans Herr Dr.
Willow Street, PA 17584
(717) 464-2771

Luzerne County Community College
Prospect St. & Midde Rd.
Nanticoke, PA 18634

Moore College of Art
20th & Parkway
Philadelphia, PA 19103
(215) 568-4515

Mount Joy Area Vocational-Technical School
RD 2
Mount Joy, PA 17552

North Montco Area Vocational-Technical School
Sumneytown Pike
Lansdale, PA 19446

Pennsylvania Academy of Fine Arts
Broad & Cherry Sts.
Philadelphia, PA 19102
(215) 972-7600

Philadelphia College of Art
Broad & Spruce Sts.
Philadelphia, PA 19102

Studio School of Art & Design
117 Chestnut St.
Philadelphia, PA 19106
(215) 592-0940

Sweetwater Art Center
417 Thorn St.
Sewickley, PA 15143

RHODE ISLAND

Hanley Education Center
91 Winter St.
Providence, RI 02903

Providence Learning Connection
769 B Hope St.
Providence, RI 02906
(401) 274-9330

Warwick Vocational-Technical Facility
Centerville Rd. & Commonwealth Ave.
Warwick, RI 02886

William M. Davies Jr. Vocational-Technical School
Jenckes Hill Rd.
Pawtucket, RI 02865

SOUTH CAROLINA

Museum School of Art
420 College St.
Greenville, SC 29601
(803) 271-7570

TENNESSEE

Harris School of Advertising Art
1109 Battlewood St.
Franklin, TN 37064
(615) 790-0407

Kingsbury Vocational-Technical Center
1328 N. Graham
Memphis, TN 38112
(901) 726-4085

Memphis Academy of Art
Overton Park
Memphis, TN 38112
(901) 726-4085

Memphis City Schools
Dept. of Vocational Education
320 Carpenter
Memphis, TN 38112

Memphis Technical High School
1266 Poplar Ave.
Memphis, TN 38104

Nichols Art Instruction
500 Paragon Mills Rd.
Suite 5F
Nashville, TN 37211

Nossi School of Art
210 Plaza Professional Building
Madison, TN 37115

Sea Isle Vocational Center
5250 Sea Isle Rd.
Memphis, TN 38117
(901) 767-4050

TEXAS

Abba Art Gallery & Studio
8822 McCann Dr.
Austin, TX 78758
(512) 258-7924

Alfred C. Glassell, Jr. School of Art
Museum of Fine Arts
PO Box 6826
Houston, TX 77005
(713) 529-7659

Art Institute of Houston
3600 Yoakum Blvd.
Houston, TX 77002
(713) 523-2564

Lowell Collins School of Art
2903 Saint St.
Houston, TX 77027
(713) 622-6962

San Antonio Art Institute
6000 N. New Braunfels Ave.
San Antonio, TX 78209

Texas Academy of Art
10802 Oasis
Houston, TX 77096

Texas State Technical Institute
PO Box 11035
Amarillo, TX 79111

Texas Vocational School
1913 S. Flores St.
San Antonio, TX 78204
(512) 225-3253

UTAH

Academy of Fine Arts
775 S. 11th E.
Salt Lake City, UT 84102

Salt Lake Art Center
20 South West Temple
Salt Lake City, UT 84101

Sevier Valley Area Vocational-Technical Center
800 W. 200 S.
Richfield, UT 84701
(801) 896-8202

Utah Technical College
1395 N. 150th E.
Provo, UT 84601
(801) 226-5000

Utah Technical College
4600 S. Redwood Rd.
Salt Lake City, UT 84131
(801) 967-4111

VERMONT

Burlington Area Vocational-Technical Center
52 Institute Rd.
Burlington, VT 05201

North Country Area Vocational-Technical Center
Veterans Ave.
Newport, VT 05855
(802) 334-7921

VIRGINIA

Arlington Career Center
816 S. Walter Reed Dr.
Arlington, VA 22204
(703) 979-6220

Jefferson Professional Institute & Holden School of Art & Design
617 W. Main St.
Charlottesville, VA 22901

North Virginia Community College
3001 N. Beauregard St.
Alexandria, VA 22311
(703) 845-6200

West Ghent Arts Alliance
1404 Gates Ave.
Norfolk, VA 23507
(804) 627-1075

WASHINGTON

Bellevue Art Museum
10310 NE 4th St.
Bellevue, WA 98004

City Art Works-Pratt Fine Arts Center
1902 S. Main
Seattle, WA 98144

Cornish Institute
710 E. Roy St.
Seattle, WA 98102

Cornish North
1501 10th Ave. E.
Seattle, WA 98102

Moldrem Atelier School of Art
1605 12th
Suite 34
Seattle, WA 98122
(206) 325-2858

New School of Visual Concepts
500 Aurora Ave. N.
Room 402
Seattle, WA 98109
(206) 623-1560

Seward Park Art Studio
5900 Lake Washington Blvd. S.
Seattle, WA 98118

Tacoma Community College
7514 Stanish Ave.
Gig Harbor, WA 98335

Tacoma Community College
5900 S. 12th St.
Tacoma, WA 98465
(206) 756-5000

WISCONSIN

Charles A. Wustum Museum of Fine Arts
2519 Northwestern Ave.
Racine, WI 53404

APPENDIX III

SCHOLARSHIPS, FELLOWSHIPS, GRANTS AND LOANS

Following are a number of organizations that offer financial support for art students. There are many other local groups that award scholarships of various kinds, from individual colleges and universities to service organizations such as Rotary or the Lions Club. Be sure to check with the financial aid officer of the school you hope to attend, as well as your guidance or placement counselor.

Cooper Union for the Advancement of Science and Art
41 Cooper Square
New York, NY 10003
(212) 254-2629
   One thousand free-tuition scholarships for those who wish to attend Cooper Union.

Education Council of the Graphic Arts Industry
Graphic Arts Technical Foundation
4615 Forbes Ave.
Pittsburgh, PA 15213
(412) 621-6941
   Forty-five scholarships of from $200 to $1,000 for students who plan to major in graphic arts.

Japanese American Citizens League
1765 Sutter St.
San Francisco, CA 94115
(415) 921-5225
   Scholarships of from $350 to $5,000 for JACL members or persons of Japanese descent who plan to study art.

Kappa Pi Honorary Art Fraternity
PO Box 7843 Midfield
Birmingham, AL 35228
(205) 428-4540
   Awards two or three $500 scholarships to college students who are members of the fraternity.

Massachusetts State Federation of Women's Clubs
148 President's Lane
Quincy, MA 02169
(617) 471-3212
   Half-tuition scholarships for Massachusetts high school seniors planning to major in art; $350 scholarships for Massachusetts high school seniors planning to attend art school.

New Jersey State Federation of Women's Clubs
55 Clifton Ave.
New Brunswick, NJ 08901
(201) 249-5474
   Three $450 scholarships for women New Jersey residents studying art at Douglass College.

Scholastic, Inc.
730 Broadway
New York, NY 10003
(212) 505-3406
   Numerous scholarships for high school students planning to study art.

Stacey Foundation
PO Box 2
Quemado, NM 87829
   Various scholarships for students planning to study the classical or conservative tradition of art.

UNICO International, Inc.
72 Burroughs Pl.
Bloomfield, NJ 07003
(201) 748-9144
   A $500 scholarship for a high school senior planning to study art history.

Virginia Museum
Boulevard & Grove Ave.
Richmond, VA 23221
(804) 257-0824
   Scholarships of $4,000 for persons born in Virginia (or who have resided there for five of the past ten years) who wish to study art.

APPENDIX IV

ORGANIZATIONS AND ASSOCIATIONS

Listed below are some major organizations and associations for persons interested in careers in art. These groups can be extremely useful resources for the individual, providing information, contacts and support.

Keep in mind, however, that there are hundreds of local and regional art groups that might be equally helpful to people interested in art and art careers—museum associations and auxiliaries, city art leagues, state and county art guilds and the like. Be sure to check into such organizations in your area.

American Art Therapy Association
505 E. Hawley St.
Mundelein, IL 60060
(312) 949-6064

American Artists Professional League
47 Fifth Ave.
New York, NY 10003
(212) 475-6650

American Institute for Conservation of Historical and Artistic Works
3545 Williamsburg La. NW
Washington, DC 20008
(202) 364-1036

American Library Association
50 E. Huron St.
Chicago, IL 60611
(312) 541-8084

American Society of Artists
PO Box 1326
Palatine, IL 60078
(312) 991-4748

American Society of Psychopathology of Expression
3811 O'Hara St.
Pittsburgh, PA 15213
(412) 624-2132

Art and Antique Dealers League of America
39 Glen Byron Ave.
Nyack, NY 10960
(914) 358-6709

Art Dealers Association of America
575 Madison Ave.
New York, NY 10022
(212) 940-8590

Art Directors Club
250 Park Ave. So.
New York, NY 10003
(212) 674-0500

Art Information Center
280 Broadway
New York, NY 10007
(212) 227-0282

Art Museum Association of America
270 Sutter St.
San Francisco, CA 94108

Association for Computer Art and Design Education
88 Garfield Ave.
Madison, NJ 07940
(201) 377-9333

Association of Art Museum Directors
1130 Sherbrooke St. W.
Montreal, PQ, Canada H3G 1G1
(514) 842-3832

Association of Artist-Run Galleries
164 Mercer St.
New York, NY 10012
(212) 226-3107

Association of Professional Art Advisers
PO Box 2485
New York, NY 10163
(212) 645-7320

College Art Association of America
149 Madison Ave.
New York, NY 10016
(212) 889-2113

Drawing Society
401 Seventh Ave.
New York, NY 10001
(212) 563-4822

Independent Curators, Inc.
799 Broadway
New York, NY 10003
(212) 254-8200

National Antique and Art Dealers Association of America
15 E. 57th St.
New York, NY 10022
(212) 355-0636

National Art Dealers Association
5669 Friendship Station
Washington, DC 20016
(202) 537-1000

National Art Education Association
1916 Association Drive
Reston, VA 22091
(703) 860-8000

National Art Materials Trade Association
178 Lakeview Ave.
Clifton, NJ 07011
(201) 546-6400

National Association of Private Art Foundations
600 New Hampshire Ave. NW
Washington, DC 20037
(202) 965-4150

National Association of Women Artists
41 Union Square West
New York, NY 10003
(212) 675-1616

National Auctioneers Association
8880 Ballentine
Overland Park, KS 66214
(913) 541-8084

Professional Picture Framers
  Association
4305 Sarellen Road
Richmond, VA 23231
(804) 226-0430

Public Relations Society of America
845 Third Ave.
New York, NY 10022
(212) 826-1750

Society of Illustrators
128 E. 63rd St.
New York, NY 10021

Visual Artists and Galleries Association
141 Fifth Ave.
New York, NY 10010
(212) 505-2280

Women's Caucus for Art
Moore College of Art
20th & The Parkway
Philadelphia, PA 19103
(215) 854-9022

APPENDIX V

BIBLIOGRAPHY

SELECTED ART PERIODICALS

ACA Update
American Council for the Arts
570 Seventh Ave.
New York, NY 10018
(212) 354-6655

ACUCAA Bulletin
Association of College, University and
Community Arts Administrators
6225 University Ave.
Madison, WI 53705-1099
(608) 233-7400

African Arts
University of California, Los Angeles
African Studies Center
405 Hilgard Ave.
Los Angeles, CA 90024
(213) 825-3686

Aha! Hispanic Arts News
Association of Hispanic Arts
200 E. 87th St.
New York, NY 10028
(212) 369-7054

American Artist
1515 Broadway
New York, NY 10036
(212) 764-7300

American Artist Business Letter
1515 Broadway
New York, NY 10036
(212) 764-7300

American Craft
American Craft Council
401 Park Ave. South
New York, NY 10016
(212) 696-0710

American Indian Art
7314 E. Osborn Dr.
Scottsdale, AZ 85251
(602) 994-5445

American Institute for Conservation Journal
American Institute for Conservation of
Historic and Artistic Works
3545 Williamsburg Ln., NW
Washington, DC 20008
(202) 364-1036

American Review
15 Burchfield Ave.
Cranford, NJ 07016
(201) 276-6222

ARC—The Rural Arts Newsletter
Rural Arts Services
Box 1547
Mendocino, CA 95460
(707) 937-4494

Archives of American Art Journal
Smithsonian Institution
Archives of American Art
Washington, DC 20560
(202) 357-2781

Art & Antiques
Allison Publications, Inc.
89 Fifth Ave.
New York, NY 10003
(212) 206-7050

Art and Artists
Foundation for the Community of Artists
280 Broadway
New York, NY 10007
(212) 227-3770

Art & Auction
Auction Guild
250 W. 57th St.
New York, NY 10019
(212) 582-5633

Art/Antiques Investment Report
Wall Street Reports Publishing Corp.
120 Wall St.
New York, NY 10005
(212) 416-2116

Art Bulletin
College Art Association of America
149 Madison Ave.
New York, NY 10016
(212) 889-2113

Art Business News
Myers Publishing Co., Inc.
60 Ridgeway Plaza
Stamford, CT 06905
(203) 356-1745

Art Com: Contemporary Art Communications
Contemporary Arts Press
Box 3123
Rincon Annex
San Francisco, CA 94119
(415) 431-7672

Art Express
Art Express Ltd.
Box 800
Canal St. Station
New York, NY 10013
(212) 661-3043

Art in America
480 Madison Avenue
New York, NY 10021
(212) 734-9797

Art Institute of Chicago Museum Studies
Art Institute of Chicago
Michigan Ave. at Adams St.
Chicago, IL 60603
(312) 962-7600

Art Journal
College Art Association of America,
Inc.
149 Madison Ave.
New York, NY 10016
(212) 889-2113

Art New England
353 Washington St.
Brighton, MA 02135
(617) 782-3008

**Art Now, USA National Art Museum
and Gallery Guide**
Art Now, Inc.
320 Bonnie Burn Rd.
Box 219
Scotch Plains, NJ 07076
(201) 322-8333

Art Papers
Atlanta Art Papers, Inc.
972 Peachtree St.
Suite 214, Box 77348
Atlanta, GA 30357
(404) 885-1273

Art Product News
In-Art Publishing Co.
Drawer 117
St. Petersburg, FL 33731
(813) 821-6064

Art Students League News
Art Students League of New York
215 W. 57th St.
New York, NY 10019
(212) 247-4510

Art/World
Arts Review, Inc.
1295 Madison Ave.
New York, NY 10128
(212) 876-5159

Artforum
65 Bleecker St.
New York, NY 10012
(212) 475-4000

Artnews
5 W. 37th St.
New York, NY 10018
(212) 398-1690

Arts Magazine
Art Digest Co.
23 E. 26th St.
New York, NY 10010
(212) 685-8500

Arts Quarterly
New Orleans Museum of Art
Box 29123
New Orleans, LA 70179
(504) 488-2631

Arts Review
National Endowment for the Arts, Public
Information Office
Washington, DC 20506
(202) 682-5400

Artweek
1628 Telegraph
Oakland, CA 94612
(415) 763-0422

Aviso
American Association of Museums
1055 Thomas Jefferson St., NW
Washington, DC 20007
(202) 338-5300

Bomb
New Art Publications
177 Franklin St.
New York, NY 10013
(212) 431-3943

CAA Newsletter
College Art Association of America
149 Madison Ave.
New York, NY 10016
(212) 889-2113

Clarion
Museum of American Folk Art
125 West 55th St.
New York, NY 10019
(212) 581-2475

Cleveland Museum of Art Bulletin
Cleveland Museum of Art, Publications
Dept.
11150 East Blvd.
Cleveland, OH 44106
(216) 421-7340

**Columbia-V. L.A. Journal of Law & the
Arts**
Columbia University, School of Law
Volunteer Lawyers for the Arts
1560 Broadway, Suite 711
New York, NY 10036
(212) 575-1150

Connoisseur
Hearst Magazines
250 W. 55th St.
New York, NY 10019
(212) 262-5700

Corporate Artnews
Artnews Associates
5 W. 37th St.
New York, NY 10018
(212) 398-1690

Craft International
Craft International Publications, Inc.
247 Centre St.
New York, NY 10013-3216
(212) 925-7320

Curator
American Museum of Natural History
79th St. and Central Park West
New York, NY 10024
(212) 873-1498

Design for Arts in Education
Heldref Publications
4000 Albemarle St., N.W.
Washington, DC 20016
(202) 362-6445

Design Quarterly
MIT Press, Journals Division
28 Carleton St.
Cambridge, MA 02142
(617) 253-2889

Detroit Institute of Arts Bulletin
Detroit Institute of Arts
5200 Woodward Ave.
Detroit, MI 48202
(313) 833-7960

Dialogues: An Art Journal
Opportunities for the Arts
Box 2572
Columbus, OH 43216-2572
(614) 221-4300

Drawing
Drawing Society, Inc.
401 Seventh Ave., No. 179
New York, NY 10001-2050
(212) 563-4822

Empirical Study of the Arts
Baywood Publishing Co.
120 Marine St., Box D
Farmingdale, NY 11735
(516) 249-2464

Evaluator
International Society of Fine Arts
Appraisers, Ltd.
Box 280
River Forest, IL 60305
(312) 848-3340

Fiberarts
Nine Press
50 College St.
Asheville, NC 28801
(704) 253-0468

High Performance
Astro Artz
240 S. Broadway, 5th Floor
Los Angeles, CA 90012
(213) 687-7362

**Houston, Texas, Museum of Fine Arts
Bulletin**
Museum of Fine Arts, Houston
Box 6826
1001 Bissonet
Houston, TX 77624
(713) 526-1361

IFAR Reports
International Foundation for Art Research, Inc.
46 E. 70th St.
New York, NY 10021
(212) 879-1780

International Bulletin for Photographic Documentation of the Visual Arts
University of Michigan
Ann Arbor, MI 48109
(313) 764-1817

International Center of Medieval Art Newsletter
International Center of Medieval Art
The Cloisters
Fort Tryon Park
New York, NY 10040
(212) 928-1146

International Sculpture
International Sculpture Center
1050 Potomac St., N.W.
Washington, DC 20007
(202) 965-6066

Journal of Aesthetics and Art Criticism
American Society for Aesthetics
Temple University
Philadelphia, PA 19122
(215) 787-8101

Leonardo: Art, Science and Technology
Pergamon Press, Inc., Journals Division
Maxwell House
Fairview Park
Elmsford, NY 10523
(914) 592-7700

Los Angeles Institute of Contemporary Art Journal
Los Angeles Institute of Contemporary Art
9021 Melrose Ave.
Los Angeles, CA 90069
(213) 276-0070

Master Drawings
Master Drawings Association, Inc.
33 E. 36th St.
New York, NY 10016
(212) 685-0008

Metropolitan Museum of Art Bulletin
Metropolitan Museum of Art
Fifth Ave. and 82nd St.
New York, NY 10028
(212) 535-7710

Midwest Museums Conference Quarterly
Field Museum of Natural History
Roosevelt Rd. at Lake Shore Dr.
Chicago, IL 60605
(312) 922-9410

Museologist
Mid-Atlantic Association of Museums
c/o Dr. Robert Ott
273 Chambers Building
Pennsylvania State University
University Park, PA 16802
(814) 865-4700

Museum News
American Association of Museums
1055 Thomas Jefferson St., N.W.
Washington, DC 20007
(202) 338-5300

Museum Studies Journal
John F. Kennedy University
Center for Museum Studies
1717 17th St.
San Francisco, CA 94103
(415) 626-1787

NAMTA News & Views
National Art Materials Trade Association
178 Lakeview Ave.
Clifton, NJ 07011
(201) 546-6400

National Arts Guide
National Arts Guide, Inc.
209 Lake Shore Dr.
Chicago, IL 60611
(312) 642-9001

New Art Examiner
Chicago New Art Association
300 W. Grand, Suite 620
Chicago, IL 60610-4106
(312) 836-0330

Neworld
Inner-City Cultural Center
1309 S. New Hampshire Ave.
Los Angeles, CA 90006
(213) 387-1161

Northwest Arts
538 N.E. 98th St.
Seattle, WA 98125
(206) 524-2146

October
MIT Press
28 Carleton St.
Cambridge, MA 02142
(617) 253-2889

Philadelphia Museum of Art Bulletin
Philadelphia Museum of Art
Box 7646
Philadelphia, PA 19101
(215) 763-8100

Praxis: A Journal of Cultural Criticism
Dickson Art Center
UCLA
Los Angeles, CA 90024
(213) 825-4321

Primitive Art Newsletter
Irwin Hersey Associates
Box 536, Ansonia Station
New York, NY 10023
(212) 966-6866

Print Collector's Newsletter
16 E. 82nd St.
New York, NY 10028
(212) 628-2654

St. Louis Art Museum Bulletin
St. Louis Art Museum
Forest Park
Saint Louis, MO 63110
(314) 721-0067

School Arts
Davis Publications, Inc.
50 Portland St.
Printers Building
Worcester, MA 01608
(617) 754-7201

Sculpture Review
National Sculpture Society
15 E. 26th St.
New York, NY 10010
(212) 889-6960

Society for Folk Arts Preservation Newsletter
Society for Folk Arts Preservation, Inc.
308 E. 79th St.
New York, NY 10021
(212) 734-4503

Sotheby's Newsletter
Sotheby's
1334 York Ave.
New York, NY 10021
(212) 606-7000

Southwest Art
9 Greenway Plaza
Houston, TX 77046
(713) 850-0990

Studies in Art Education
National Art Education Association
1916 Association Dr.
Reston, VA 22091
(703) 860-8000

Technology & Conservation of Art, Architecture & Antiques
Technology Organization, Inc.
1 Emerson Place
Boston, MA 02114
(617) 227-8581

Upfront
339 Lafayette St.
New York, NY 10012
(212) 420-8196

Virginia Museum of Fine Arts Bulletin
Virginia Museum of Fine Arts
Blvd. and Grove Ave.
Richmond, VA 23221
(804) 257-0534

Walters Art Gallery Bulletin
Walters Art Gallery
600 N. Charles St.
Baltimore, MD 21201
(301) 547-9000

Washington International Arts Letter
Box 9005
Washington, DC 20003
(202) 328-1900

Western Art Digest
812 S. Tejon St.
Colorado Springs, CO 80903
(303) 635-9370

White Walls: A Magazine of Writings by Artists
Box 8204
Chicago, IL 60680
(312) 274-4699

Winterthur Portfolio: A Journal of American Material Culture
University of Chicago Press
5801 S. Ellis Ave.
Chicago, IL 60637
(312) 962-7600

Woman's Art Journal
7008 Sherwood Dr.
Knoxville, TN 37919
(615) 584-7467

Women in the Arts Bulletin/Newsletter
Women in the Arts Foundation, Inc.
325 Spring St., Room 200
New York, NY 10013
(212) 691-0988

BOOKS

Berlye, Milton K., *Selling Your Art Work*. Cranbury, NJ: A.S. Barnes, 1973.

Brough, James, **Auction!** Indianapolis: Bobbs-Merrill, 1963.
Caplin, Lee E., ed., *The Business of Art*. Englewood Cliffs, NJ: Prentice-Hall, 1982.

Career Associates, *Career Choices for Students of Art*. New York: Walker, 1985.

Casewit, Curtis W., *Making a Living in the Fine Arts*. New York: Macmillan, 1981.

Chamberlain, Betty, *The Artist's Guide to His Market*. New York: Watson-Guptill, 1975.

Cochrane, Diane, *This Business of Art*. New York: Watson-Guptill, 1978.

Corwen, Leonard, *There's a Job for You in . . .* Piscataway, NJ: New Century, 1983.

Fromme, Babbette B., *Curator's Choice: An Introduction to the Art Museums of the United States*. New York: Crown Publishers, 1981.

Gould, Christine, *Consider Your Options: Business Opportunities for Liberal Arts Graduates*. Washington, DC: Association of American Colleges, 1983.

Holden, Donald, *Art Career Guide*. New York: Watson-Guptill, 1983.

Lobb, Charlotte, *Exploring Careers Through Voluntarism*. New York: Richards Rosen Press, 1979.

Meyer, Karl E., *The Art Museum: Power, Money and Ethics*. New York: William Morrow, 1981.

Montaperto, Nicki, *The Freelancer's Career Book*. New York: Arco Publishers, 1983.

Munschauer, John L., *Jobs for English Majors and Other Smart People*. Princeton, NJ: Peterson's Guides, 1982.

Sherman, Lila, *Art Museums of America*. New York: William Morrow, 1980.

U.S. Department of Labor, *Career Opportunities in Art Museums, Zoos, and Other Interesting Places*. Washington, DC: U.S. Department of Labor, 1980.

Walker, John, *Expert's Choice*. New York: Stewart Tabori and Chang, 1983.

INDEX